Older Man/between two _____ ... ... that transcends time and space by constantly evoking memories of other lifetimes spent in similar mutual devotion.

In the timelessness of this relationship the archetypal pair of master and disciple with its characteristic erotic charge appears here in a modern garb where the disciple often surpasses his master in relational sensitivity and practical wisdom. The common ground of this uneven pair is an unwavering loyalty and a deep, passionate love for one another where sexuality becomes the glue that binds two souls together in an inseparable union.

Of all the good books Joseph Dispenza has written this is his best. Love seems to have opened the door to poetic expression and taken him to new heights of visual evocativeness in his writing. In one courageous leap of faith he has plunged himself into his own depth of human vulnerability where the specter of social stigma, sickness, old age and loss of life looms large against the background of a loving relationship with a much younger partner. The honesty that was required to write this groundbreaking book is deserving of the greatest respect.

> Sabine Lucas, Ph.D., Jungian Analyst, author
> of *Past Life Dreamwork: Healing the Soul through
> Understanding Karmic Patterns*

This is a compelling story, beautifully rendered, that will enlighten and surprise you about a topic that you might even consider a mild taboo. Not after you read this gripping and persuasive book.

> Susan Page, author of *The 8 Essential Traits of Couples Who Thrive* and *Why Talking Is Not Enough: Loving Actions That Will Transform Your Marriage*

Older Man/Younger Man is a revealing and insightful presentation of sex, romance, and relationship as stages of psychological and spiritual development. Explaining the dynamics of a common, but unconventional model of male bonding, Joseph Dispenza offers deep wisdom about the nature of religion, consciousness, and time.

> Toby Johnson, author of *Gay Spirituality: The Role of Gay Identity in the Transformation of Human Consciousness*

Redemption comes in many forms. We like to think that we do life, but the truth is that it does us. Joseph Dispenza has given us a tale of deep authenticity, of how the sacred came to him in the form of a loving relationship, and how it transformed his life. 'God' is not elsewhere, he seems to be saying; it's the daily process of living itself.

> Morris Berman, author of *The Reenchantment of the World* and *Coming to Our Senses: Body and Spirit in the Hidden History of the West*

Older Man/Younger Man is a brave, groundbreaking book. It's not *just* a gay man's story; it is a stunningly beautiful and universal story of love, courage, and faith. The author's compelling narrative pierces the heart with fundamental truths: love transcends age, sexual orientation, and religious conditioning; love heals; love is timeless; love binds us all.

This book invites us to more closely examine the transformational power of love, no matter where we find it, no matter the age, skin color, religious beliefs, or sexual orientation of the bearer.

I applaud Dispenza for his courage and honesty. He boldly paves the way for generations to come. I am a better person from reading this riveting story. It forever changed how I view love. I couldn't put it down!

Robin Easton, author of *Naked in Eden: My Adventure and Awakening in the Australian Rainforest*

Other Books by Joseph Dispenza

God On Your Own

On Silence

The Way of the Traveler

The Magical Realism of Alyce Frank

Live Better Longer

The Serigraphs of Doug West

Will Shuster: A Santa Fe Legend

The House of Alarcon (novel)

Advertising the American Woman

Freeze Frame: A History of American Film

Re–Runs: Cinema on Television

Forgotten Patriot

Older Man

Younger Man

Older Man
Younger Man

A Love Story

Joseph Dispenza

www.oldermanyoungerman.com

Dedication

Once again, for Michael Charles Herbert

Copyright © 2011 Joseph Dispenza
All rights reserved.

ISBN: 1460956982
ISBN-13: 9781460956984

*Whatever our souls are made of, his
and mine are the same.*

Emily Brontë

Foreword

April 2009: In a Mexican Monastery

I wonder what these monks would think if they knew I was here working on a book about my love for a much younger man, and how that love has saved my soul. Love of men for other men is not unheard of in monasteries, of course. I have spent many lifetimes as a monk, some of them loving younger men. I have spent part of this lifetime, eight years, in monastic life, and had my share of crushes and indescribable longings and heartbreaks over young men so beautiful that they seemed to have dropped to earth from heaven.

The monks here would forgive this double scandal of the romance between an older man and a younger man, surely, as they would forgive just about anything else set before them. Besides, there may be a tradition of mentor-student love within their sacred ranks: some believe that Michelangelo, himself a lover of youths, depicted it in all its religious glory for a knowing clergy in the famous panel above the Sistine Chapel in the Vatican—a graybeard God touching the finger of the nude young Adam, bringing him to life.

I am in this remote Benedictine *monasterio de silencio* in Mexico's cactus and thorn tree-strewn high desert reviewing what I wrote about Mike and me, trying to see whether I left anything important out—and whether I should remove anything that might be better left out. Reading these pages is like reading the tea leaves of the past: it is the opposite of fortunetelling—it is past-telling, trying to see clearly who I am and who he is and who we are together in the puzzle pieces, the hieroglyphics of another time, even though the time was only a few years ago, almost as recent as yesterday. I am even trying to decide whether to tell this story at all.

Before I met Mike and began to explore the mysteries of relationship with him I had closed the door entirely to that part of me that felt drawn toward younger men. I had experienced rejection from the objects of my affection and abuse, whether verbal or outright physical, from others—even those who thought it was acceptable to love men, but *not* all right to love much younger men.

Mike had similar experiences in his search for an appropriate mate. He had boyfriends his own age who adored him, and girlfriends, for that matter, but their attentions left him frustrated and unsatisfied. When he tried to pursue older men, he usually encountered only those he charitably ended up calling "creeps." We both had nearly given up hope of finding anyone to love before we found each other.

We are many years apart in age: I am thirty years and eight months older than Mike; I am a couple of years older than his parents. I was fifty-five when we met; he was twenty-five. This age disparity gives our bond a kind of built-in early expiration date which plays like the hum of the stars behind the nights and days of our romance. Bittersweet is the word that comes to mind: sweet our time together, bitter its cruel foreshortening.

That aside, we consider our relationship ordinary in most ways. We live together in a big house, we have a dog and a car, we share our financial resources, we work together in side-by-side offices at careers with similar goals, we take trips together, we are monogamous. We take pleasure in each other's bodies often and with ardor.

Ordinary or unusual, what most makes me want to tell the story of this partnership of ours is my evolving understanding of it as my spiritual path. It has been my deliverance from a life of bitter loneliness, an empty, arid, Godless place within. But more than that, it has allowed me to live open and honest and unafraid. When Mike came into my life, a new turn in the path began for me that led back to my spiritual center.

And so, in this bare monastery cell, in the predawn chill of this day, listening to the soft shuffle of the celibate monks on their way to chant the Morning Hours, I am contemplating the miracle of how the separate journeys of two souls have come together into one pilgrimage of love—and considering how love heals shame, as it heals everything else.

Chapter One

Pan is in the forest. Pan comes to us with his pipes, urging us on to ecstasy. We bring up the gods in this moment, as we had so long ago on some grassy hillside overlooking a sapphire blue harbor somewhere in the Island Kingdom, sometime before Pericles. I am a tutor, you are my treasured student; you reach out your hand and touch my beard and I reach my hand down there between your thighs, as in the drawing on the urn in your father's library, the one beside the shelf that holds the scrolls of love poetry. Your beauty delights me. How fortunate to have found you, and for you to have found me in the agora that day, walking with the senior students, you stopping to bind up your sandal, waving your racing friends ahead to give you more time to stare at me staring at you. A cloud of white sheep appears on the opposite hillside, and now a prancing he-goat, and again I remember, just before I turn back to your exquisite young arms, Pan and his song.

Wednesday, December 19, 2007

By now, the graceful arches and church domes and cobblestone streets of San Miguel de Allende in central Mexico, quaint and exotic to visitors, are as familiar to us as if we had been born here. The town was founded in 1542. Virtually unchanged for the last two hundred years, it has the charming feel of a sleepy old Spanish or Italian mountain town. We expatriates—probably seven-thousand in a town of seventy-thousand people—live here in another culture and in another century, as well: the first time I looked out my office window to see two burros loaded down with firewood ambling down the lane on the way to a home delivery, I welled up with emotion.

I feel tired this afternoon at the office, exhausted, really. I finish seeing clients at about the same time as Mike, and I suggest that we go to one of our favorite restaurants for a drink and dinner. Ordinarily, we would hop on our motor scooters—motorcycles and scooters are a perfect way to get around San Miguel, with its narrow streets and scarce parking spaces—but this "winter" night is mild, in the sixties, and the restaurant is only four blocks away, so we walk. I am thinking that the stroll might take the edge off my fatigue.

At well over six feet, Mike is taller than me by almost five inches. When we walk together in San Miguel, I take the thin strip of sidewalk that runs between high plastered walls and narrow cobblestone streets, and he takes the street, so we are even in height. Tonight, he is in a good mood, anticipating our trip the next day. He gathers his long, honey-colored hair, which has been flying around in the breeze, and ties it back into a ponytail. He ties only the middle section back, so that some of his hair hangs down on each side, making him look like Legolas the Elf in *The Lord of the Rings*. His slender, dancer's body does a little skip every few steps. I, heavier than Mike and older—he is thirty-four; I am sixty-five—seem to plod along by comparison.

If he is Legolas, I am, or so I have been told, the Sean Connery of late middle age, but with hair. I had never seen the resemblance until a Japanese caricature artist in San Francisco a few years ago was convinced I was the movie star and began sketching me, attracting a small crowd of tourists who debated among themselves whether I was or was not "Shaw-Collery," as the artist insisted. When I tried to pay him for the sketch, he refused, saying that it was his way of thanking me for years of entertaining him on the screen. Maybe it is my close-cropped salt-and-pepper beard that caught the caricaturist's imagination.

Tomorrow we are to leave our home in San Miguel to visit Mike's parents in the United States for Christmas. In spite of the effort involved—we will need to drive an hour to get on a bus, then bus another four hours to get on a plane, then another plane—I am looking forward to the trip, which will give both of us the opportunity to rest and do nothing, to recover from the volatile dramas of the past few months.

I am also looking forward to reconnecting with Mike's parents, whom I genuinely like and with whom, in many ways, I have more in common than I do with Mike. They live in San Antonio, Texas now, the most recent of a dozen relocations around the country on military assignments. The first time I met them was around Christmastime nine years ago, four months after Mike entered my life. To my surprise—and great relief—we connected at that time and have been friends ever since.

Mike and I came to this small sixteenth-century Spanish Colonial hill town seven years ago, along with our friend, Beverly Nelson, to create a facility for personal growth and healing. LifePath Center was the result, a place where we offer retreats, workshops and classes, and see private clients. Mike is a massage therapist and body worker, on his way to becoming a naturopathic doctor. I am a spiritual counselor. Beverly, who is our housemate as well as our business partner, is a smart, lively redhead with thirty-five years experience as a psychologist.

We walk through the *Jardin*, the town's tree-shrouded "garden," main square, and outdoor salon, where religious and civil pageants are staged and where, on rare non-fiesta days, people simply walk about and mingle. A small nineteenth century bandstand sits at the heart of the park, which is planted with rich green jasmine shrubs and, at this time of the year, long patches of velvety, deep red poinsettia—*nochebuena*, in Spanish, literally "good night," the name for Christmas Eve. Old-fashioned cast iron benches painted white border the walkways. The *Jardin* is anchored by the gothic salmon-hued *Parroquia* church, a towering fanciful structure built in 1683, which seems to belong more to the Barcelona of Gaudi than to San Miguel.

At the restaurant, a cozy gringo hangout, I order a *ceviche*, raw fish marinated in lime juice, forgetting in my drained state that we are in the high desert, far away from the ocean and fresh fish. For an hour or two I am somewhat revived, but by the time we get back to the house the exhaustion returns—and I have yet to pack. I am feeling overwhelmed, but manage to get my things together and crawl into bed.

During the night, I have to get up to pee several times. My sleep is restless and disturbed. My legs, for some reason, cannot get comfortable. I try to remind myself to tell Mike about this in the morning. I will even make fun of it, I think, by saying that I may have Restless Leg Syndrome, something we have seen on a TV commercial and joked about as an improbable, maybe imaginary disease.

༄

Ten Years Before

We saw each other for the first time in a tiny, funky coffee bar in Las Vegas, a small old town in northern New Mexico, seventy miles east of Santa Fe. The Great Plains end and the Rocky Mountains start at Las Vegas. In its heyday, the last years of the nineteenth century, rail travelers from the East used to stop there, as well, rich families on their way from Chicago to winter homes in Pasadena and well-heeled Philadelphians wanting to take the waters at nearby Montezuma Castle, a huge, rambling, turreted, and gabled Victorian fantasy on a hill outside town. In the 1870s Billy the Kid shot someone on the tree-shaded plaza in Las Vegas—besides the railroad, it is the town's claim to fame.

On the morning of that August day I had had my car serviced for the scheduled oil-change and checkup. Driving back through town to my house in Santa Fe, I thought I would take the rest of the day off. I came to an intersection on the north-south axis through town. I could turn left and go up to Taos, or I could turn right and head east to Las Vegas. Three years before, I had spent time a few miles north of Las Vegas in the tucked-away, woodsy village of Sapello, where I studied with Hazel Parcells, a centenarian practitioner of natural healing. I wrote a book about my experience with her, *Live Better Longer*. Hazel had passed away at the age of 106 in 1996, and I had not been back up there since. I flicked on my right turn-signal, deciding almost absentmindedly on Las Vegas.

On the way up Highway 25, through gorgeous mountain passes, I reflected on how good I felt about my life. I was fifty-five years old and in excellent health. I had a few good friends, among them a former student of mine and his new wife. With them, I shared a comfortable adobe house in a fashionable area of Santa Fe. I was not rich, but I was not poor, either. I was living on savings and occasional little windfalls from magazine writing. I was more solidly myself and at peace than I think I had ever been.

Except that I did not have the one thing I most craved in my life: a romantic relationship. For some reason, probably because I felt age creeping up on me, the need for a long-term relationship was becoming urgent. Relationship had never come easy for me. For many years I had been closeted, even to myself, and therefore unfocused about some basic issues, such as what gender I was looking to connect with. I had fooled myself with thinking that the right "person" would enter my life at the right time—"person" was more important than male or female. It was a delusion: I knew in my heart that nothing, no one, would be right unless it was a man, and a man younger than me.

Over the two or three years before that midmorning ride to Las Vegas I must have tried a dozen ways to bring relationship to me. With my friend Snow, who had just received her degree in Spiritual Psychology, I "un-vowed" myself of promises I had made as a boy out of high school when I entered a Catholic monastery. We did a ritual to reverse the vows of Poverty, Chastity, and Obedience—vows I had left behind at the monastery gate after eight years, but apparently was still dragging around with me in adulthood.

"Do you renounce the vow of Chastity?" Snow asked me gravely, officially, over a bank of flickering candles on my bedside table. She lowered her eyes and waited, wiping a lock of black hair away from her lovely pale-skinned face.

"I do renounce it," I said finally in a choked voice, echoing with a vague memory the rite of Christian Baptism wherein one renounces Satan. Dropping my chaste past, making room for the joys of romantic love, felt like a load of bricks falling off my shoulders. For some time afterward I felt hopeful, but my bed remained empty.

Chapter Two

My spiritual journey began around the time my mother stopped going to church after her mother died. The death of my grandmother when I was eight marked the end of an era for us, the symbolic passing of the first generation of my Italian family in America. Her death came as a shock, even though she had been bedridden for six months with terminal ailments associated with diabetes, which was then still difficult to treat. My mother, the baby of her eight children, heavy-set, possessing the energy of a steam-engine, was her nurse through her final year. When she was dying, she cried out for my mother, who in turn cried out to God for help.

They carried my grandmother out of the house in the early afternoon, then brought her back in the evening, dressed and rouged, to the same bedroom where she had expired, which was now a viewing room for the three-day wake. All the children and the many uncles, aunts, and cousins who came and stationed themselves there were brokenhearted; my mother, though, was devastated. She cried a little, then her face set in a kind of stone mask of anger that she wore for a long time afterwards. It was there in her face thirty years later when she lay on her own deathbed, and I silently prayed to God for help.

Because of my grandmother's death, my mother decided to turn her back on the God who had abandoned her in her hour of need. Not only did she stop going to church, but she also became silent when any mention of God or the church came up in conversation. She made one concession to a vague, perhaps even pagan divinity. She cleared a shelf in the bedroom that had been my grandmother's, and which she now shared with my father, and made a small altar, with my grandmother's photograph, dried flowers, a holy card with a prayer to St. Teresa of Lisieux on the back, a lace doily, and a votive candle. My mother's sister, Aunt Lily, tried to talk to her about this self-exile from religion, explaining that it was not good for the children—my younger brother and me—to grow up outside the faith.

"They can go to church if they want," my mother said unconvincingly, knowing perfectly well that if it were a choice between her and God, we would choose her. Besides, for us at that age church was a bore. Aunt Lily shook her head and clicked her tongue.

Two years would pass before my mother would give an inch in the matter. My mother's negative attitude toward all things holy began to shift slightly when a new family moved into the neighborhood.

Chapter Two

The new neighbor woman, Mrs. Severino, was a workhorse and a devout Catholic. My mother connected with the workhorse aspect—she was herself a tireless scrubber of counters and straightener of rugs—and, gradually, she began to relate to Mrs. Severino's interest in church activities, which presented still another opportunity for staying busy.

After much coaxing, my mother reluctantly agreed to accompany the neighbor to a Sunday afternoon meeting of the Altar and Rosary Society. A "good Samaritan" housecleaning for sick members of the parish had been discussed. She returned home that evening trying, not too successfully, to repress her pleasure. It was the first indication my father, my brother, and I had that the household would soon experience a seismic change.

A month went by, and another Altar and Rosary Society meeting. At last, one night at the supper table, my mother nonchalantly slid into the conversation the news that she was thinking about going to church on Sunday. My brother and I looked at each other in horror: If she was thinking about going to church on Sunday, it meant that we would be going with her—and not just this Sunday, but all the Sundays of the rest of our childhoods. She might as well have said that she was thinking about murdering us with the bread knife.

Like the newly converted, my mother would throw herself into religion with enormous enthusiasm. And, like the newly converted, she would drag her family along with her into the big sacred circus. Church, after an absence of three formative years, was a revelation to me. I enjoyed the theatricality of the services—especially Solemn High Mass, with the torchbearers, the incense, the ecclesiastical costumes, the lock-step military formations of the altar boys.

The little altar in my parents' bedroom had been a curiosity—the one link, however tenuous, between my mother's flight from the divine to the larger world of religiosity. Now I was looking at real altars and witnessing real drama. With a neighbor boy, Robbie, who also was intrigued by church theatricality, I built my own altar in my grandfather's dilapidated tool shed behind the house. The shed had a distinct and heavy aroma—the smell of a barn far out in the country: sunbaked slats, straw, the weathered wooden handles of rakes and shovels and hoes, cans of motor oil, decaying newspapers. The rich scents of the shed, like the incense at church, created its own world. All during the summer following my return to religion, this was my private cathedral.

The altar in the shed was a simple affair. Robbie and I constructed it with things we pilfered from our homes. The centerpiece was a foot-long wooden crucifix, part of a "last rites" set given to my mother by the undertaker who had buried my grandmother. The Extreme Unction kit, as it was called, was a particularly good altar-starter, since it also contained two small bottles with silver caps—one bottle for holy oil, the other for holy water—and a linen napkin. To these we added candles, fresh wild roses from the bushes behind the shed, a lace-trimmed white handkerchief, and a tiny plastic statue of St. Christopher that once had adorned the dashboard of my father's Ford.

Robbie and I, during our breaks from examining how each other's penises worked, held services at the altar in the tool shed. Usually I was the priest and he was everyone else. I would approach the altar, whisper something in mock-Latin, take the plastic St. Christopher in my hands, turn around, and give Robbie a sweeping sign-of-the-cross blessing. For these services I was vested in an antique fringed Neapolitan piano cover. Robbie wore the remnants of a linen bed sheet. After the services, we went out into the weedy fields behind the shed, pulled our pants down, and resumed our inquires into each other's personal plumbing.

At some point these two activities—holding services and playing with each other's erect penises—merged into one. It happened quite naturally one day during one of our services. We agreed that at the most solemn moment of the blessing we should both get naked from the waist down. In this way we were able to combine both religious ecstasy and just plain ecstasy, allowing guilt for the one to be absolved in the high spiritual purpose of the other. Somehow, spirituality and sex were related.

By the end of that summer we had gotten bored with both the tool shed services and each other's sexual equipment, and moved on to collecting baseball cards and building mud forts. I had forgotten about the altar in the tool shed until my mother, on a hunt for missing lace doilies, discovered it and confronted me about it. I explained to her that Robbie and I had been so moved by what we were experiencing in church that we wanted to have a private home altar of our own—just as she had. She seemed satisfied.

A few weeks later my mother let it drop in conversation at supper that she had been speaking to the parish priest about me and that he thought my interest in altars might be an indication that I had a vocation to the priesthood.

༄

During the years in New Mexico, I attempted to use "spiritual" means to catch my mate. On little cards, I wrote out affirmations such as *I am enjoying a relationship with exactly the right man, I have the man of my dreams in my life, My life is fulfilled by the perfect lover,* and repeated them over and over many times a day. I imagined the object of my love in a journal devoted to my hopes for a relationship, describing him down to his shirt size and the way he smiled at me. For many months I lived with the phantom partner I tried desperately to create, even hugging his stand-in, my pillow, at night as I drifted off to an uneasy sleep.

I have heard that we can bring someone to us by various spiritual means such as the so-called Law of Attraction if we will just concentrate hard, but it did not work for me. The New Agers, of whom there were many in Santa Fe at the time I lived there, were fond of saying that we create our own reality, but I found that true only up to a point—and the point did not include a loving partnership.

Let me gather you up and eat your youth from off your lips, beautiful young man, brought to me by the cup-bearer of the great god himself. I loved you before I knew you. You hid from me in the shadows of the temple columns. I, aroused, had gone looking for you. There in the dark, behind a tree, I caught a glimpse of your hair on the sudden gust of wind, silver-struck in the white moonlight. My unbearable excitement impels me. But I waited there on the marble steps, wanting to lengthen the moment. How many times have I found you and lost you and found you again?

Chapter Three

When I arrived in Las Vegas, I stopped for a ham-and-cheese sandwich at a diner off the shady Plaza. Looking at the little round sour pickle slices that garnished the plate, I thought about my own small town, Ashtabula, Ohio, and growing up there in the 1950s. We had a diner just like this one on Main Avenue. I went there with my mother after shopping and sat across from her in a booth with red leather seats eating grilled cheese sandwiches with pickle slices the size of quarters placed neatly on the edge of the plate next to a curly leaf of lettuce. In Las Vegas, that time lived on. After lunch, I walked around the Plaza and over to the turn-of-the-century hotel that bordered one side of it. A few years before, the hotel had been renovated and restored, giving the town a brave hope for the future in the memory of a more prosperous past.

I walked down the main street, Bridge Street, to find a coffee shop. I remembered there was one place with a genuine espresso maker imported from Italy. That place, I soon discovered, had gone out of business and become a curio and card shop. But the espresso maker had survived and was now the centerpiece of a little coffee bar a few doors down.

If the 1950s had endured at the diner on the Plaza, the early 1970s were still alive at the coffee bar. The place was long and narrow, the walls hung with dark abstract paintings with little white stick-on price-tags. Four small tables and a few chairs and an old couch. I took a seat by the window. A tall, slender, serious looking young man with long light brown hair tied back in a ponytail peeked his head around the famous espresso maker. I made myself more comfortable in the chair. He came out from behind the little counter.

"Can I get a coffee?" I asked, noting a cheerful lilt in my voice.

"Sure," he said, his expression still rather serious and professional. "Do you like it strong? I can make you a 'Shot-in-the-Dark'." His hand went to a cluster of cups that were stacked upside-down on a clean white towel and turned one over.

"What's a Shot-in-the-Dark?"

"Black coffee with a shot of espresso—you'll like it," he said. Then, glancing back to me as he made his way over to the espresso machine, he said, "I'm Mike."

"Joseph," I said. My eyes surveyed more of the room, soaking in the ambience of a post-hippie world: a threadbare paisley-patterned curtain over the door to the kitchen, mismatched wood kitchen chairs, beige walls sponged with a darker tan for texture, dog-eared and yellowing copies of *High Times* and *Rolling Stone* and *Guitar World* on a thrift-store coffee-table.

The coffee, when it arrived, was delicious. I spent some time slowly sipping and savoring it, all the while looking at Mike and pretending not to be admiring his looks. A few young people came into the bar for cappuccinos. After they drifted out, Mike made me another coffee without my asking for it. I began to think that Mike was rather cute. "Cute Mike," I said to myself. Did he like men? If he liked men, did he like me?

I decided to make a move, but one that would not entirely tip my hand or scare him away. "So," I said, "what's the scene like in this town?"

"The scene?" he asked without looking up. The warm late afternoon light from the front window glowed on his face, emphasizing his fine features.

"You know, the dating scene."

"That depends," he said right away with a shrug, his expression unreadable. For a moment he seemed to be pondering what exactly he meant by his comment. I had caught him off guard. Now his face softened, the seriousness melted, the hint—just a hint—of a mischievous smile appeared.

"Actually," he said finally, "there isn't much happening up here. A few guys, some women, all nice people, but...not much happening." His eyes asked if he could sit down in the chair across from me, and I motioned for him to join me. He turned the chair around and straddled it, folding his arms on the chair back and leaning into it.

"I've had a couple of dates," he said, still dancing around the big question of his sexual preference.

"Oh? How did they go?"

He appeared to be thinking about what he wanted to say. "Fine, I guess. Well, one guy was a little creepy."

At last! I said to myself, amused by the way Cute Mike was revealing himself to me in slow, cautious stages. His candor and vulnerability were kindling a small spark in me. I felt myself shift in my chair. When I took a sip from my coffee cup, I sensed his eyes giving me a once-over.

For the next half hour we chatted about Las Vegas, about the differences between Las Vegas and Santa Fe, about people in those places. I told Mike a little about my life, how I was between things, between big projects, writing a book. He told me he had finished massage school and was looking to launch a career as a therapist, but did not know whether he could do that in Las Vegas, where there was little disposable income. He was living here because his brother was a student at Highlands University, the small state school in town; he thought they could live together and share expenses, but that had not worked out and he was living by himself in a two-room place on the other side of the river. He was twenty-five years old.

The woman whose paintings hung on the coffee bar's walls dropped in. Mike got up to talk to her. She did not want a coffee, but had just come by as a neighborly gesture and, it seemed to me, to see if any of her art had sold. When she walked out a teenage boy and his girlfriend in matching black tee-shirts and tattered jeans came in. They looked around, said something to each other, and left.

"Is this your place...or do you work here?" I asked Mike when we were alone again.

"Ray is the owner. He...didn't come in today, so I took his place. I'm not here usually." He settled back on his chair with his chin resting on his folded arms.

We talked more, then suddenly it was five-thirty. I told him I did not want to go back to Santa Fe. I would walk over to the Plaza Hotel to get a room. In this sleepy town on a sleepy August afternoon with no tourists in sight, the Plaza surely had vacancies.

"You can get a cheaper room at another place," Mike said. Then, after a few seconds, "It's clean, nice." I said that sounded good and asked him how to get there. He started giving me directions, curving his hand this way and that and making an intersection with his two index fingers. I must have had a puzzled look on my face.

"Why don't I just take you there?" he said. "I have to close up here, then we can go."

"Okay, if it's not too much trouble." An adventure was brewing. I felt a stirring in my pants.

We got into my car and dove over to the hotel, which was four streets away and which, in this tiny town, I could have found on my own. Mike said he had to run home to feed his cat, but would be back if I wanted company.

"Yes, please come back," I said, trying to mask my mounting sense of anticipation. On the hotel stoop I watched him walk away down the street and felt something I would feel again and again in the next weeks and months, and years: he was leaving me and I wondered, with a sinking heart, if he would ever come back. I had known him only for a few hours, but I was already fond of him and, crazy as it seemed, I was missing him.

He came back. About an hour later he knocked on my hotel room door. I had gone out and bought a six-pack of beer and some snacks. He didn't like beer, it turned out, and neither did I, but we munched on the snacks. I turned on the TV and we lounged on the bed trying to find something to watch.

Something about all this seemed familiar to me. It was as if I had a boyfriend, and had had him for a long time. The television droned on—people were answering questions on a quiz show, a bell rang, the audience was laughing and applauding. We stretched back on the bed and lay there side by side. I should have been nervous, but I was quite calm. When my right hand went for his left hand and held it, when I felt him respond by squeezing my hand lightly, it all seemed so natural. Moments later we were entwined in each other's hungry arms, making love.

Do you remember that hushed early evening in the ruins of Armana with the setting sun spilling on the sands like thick Bibline wine, how you came to me after I had dismissed the guards? Ah, incomparable Bithynian, I was your slave, not you mine. I ascended you, glorious flesh of my own youth, and joined the stem of you to the stem of me in a merging moment we had known so many times before—and would know again so many times—the awakening of the older man in you, the rapture of the younger man in me, together again as in ancient times, as we were in our beloved Lemuria the afternoon after your initiation, as we will be in future times on colonies of the home planet yet to come; we melt into one another to make the god of death and rebirth. Your breath on my cheek inflames me to even great heights, so that I burn myself out in you as I see you rising to me, emptying yourself in sacred generosity, making me young, oh so young again!

Chapter Four

At a little after ten we finally drifted off to sleep. I did not invite him to stay the night; in the same natural way the rest of it had unfolded, Mike simply snuggled up to the pillow, pulled himself close to me, and fell asleep. It had been a long time since I had slept with someone—I could not remember the last time. I should have been restless all night lying next to this young man I had met only hours earlier, this stranger. But I felt comfortable and relaxed lying there.

I must have turned a couple of times in my sleep, and then it was morning. I stared out the lace-draped tall Victorian window at an eastern sky starting to fill with color and remembered that I had slept with a beautiful young man the night before, and he was still here, he was asleep next to me.

I slipped out of bed quietly, pulled on my Levis and tee-shirt, and went downstairs to the hotel's little restaurant. A few minutes later I got back up to the room balancing two Styrofoam cups of hot coffee. Mike was just waking up, stretching and looking around for his clothes.

"I didn't know if you wanted cream and sugar," I said, setting the cups down on the nightstand.

"It's okay—I have to go," he said abruptly.

His announcement was such a disappointment that I felt I had been punctured and the air let out of me. I had thought we might spend some time in the morning in bed, then in the afternoon go out and have a leisurely meal before I drove back to Santa Fe. I asked him for his phone number.

"I don't have a phone," he said. "Well, it's the landlord's phone and I don't use it unless there's an emergency." He pulled on his jeans and white socks.

"How can I reach you?" I asked, suddenly worried that I might never see him again. I plopped down on the edge of the bed.

"Oh, Las Vegas is a small town," he replied enigmatically.

Before I could frame another question, he came up to me and kissed me on the lips—a fleeting reminder of our night of love—and the next moment was out the door.

I spent the rest of the morning trying to overcome my feelings of loss. Was this going to be like all the rest of my sexual encounters over the past few years? Was this the same brief coming together followed by an irrevocable parting I had experienced almost all my adult life? Was I to be denied what so many people, so many of my friends, enjoyed easily and many times over through their lives—the great heart-opening of relationship?

After an agitated breakfast of scrambled eggs and flour tortillas at the hotel restaurant, I walked the streets a bit. Maybe I was thinking that, since Mike had said Las Vegas was a small town, he would be there waiting for me around the corner or walking out of a store. At last, I returned to the hotel, checked out, and drove back to the coffee bar.

Ray, the owner who had been absent the day before, was there with three or four customers. Ray had a shaved head and the taut thirty-something body of a mountain-bike athlete. When I asked him about Mike, he gave me a look that seemed to know everything that had happened between Mike and me since yesterday. Small towns are like tribes, I thought; when one person does something, everyone looped into the tribal mind automatically knows about it.

"No, I haven't seen Mike this morning," he said, mustering a smile. "He's not usually here, you know. Yesterday he came in and said I looked tired, so he told me to go home. I did. I really needed the day off. He didn't even want me to pay him anything. That's the kind of guy Mike is."

Ray looked me in the eye as he spoke trying, it seemed to me, to see what kind of guy I was, as well. Was there anything in what he was saying the faint suggestion of a sales pitch?

I asked Ray for directions to Mike's house and drove over to where I thought it was, but could not find him. I returned to the coffee bar and wrote Mike a long note, starting with "CuteMike—"

"I couldn't find you," I wrote. "I want to invite you to a party I'm giving in Santa Fe on Saturday. Call me?" I wrote down the toll-free number I used for business to make it easier for him to call—from Las Vegas, it would be long-distance.

When I drove out of town and got back on the highway that Thursday morning, I did not know whether I would ever see Mike again. My feelings were all over the place, torn between the exquisite and graceful lovemaking of the night before and the sense of loss when I could not find him in the morning. As far as I knew, everything that happened to me in that little town might have been just a dream.

I come home to people who have no memory of where I have been, who I have been—standing against an ancient arch in the half-light of a Roman dusk, waiting for the promise of pleasure to bloom, getting hard in my pants, looking, looking. I embrace who I am and who I was—and who I am becoming. I hold onto whoever is in the bed of my imagination, turning over the person to see the face: did we meet last night, and did we... make love? I forget; tell me. Speak to me before you yawn again, scratch yourself, open your lovely eyes upon the new day. Young god of my imagination, I grunt your name in a spasm, holding you, rubbing my wetness on my stomach like a salve, a balm to heal my loneliness. Alone in my dreams, with the skin next to my skin separate, oh, so separate.

Chapter Four

Birds sing in the trees outside my house here in Santa Fe—it is so quiet that one can almost see souls wandering around. The Telephone Man comes to the door and says he has been talking to "the buried people" all morning. I take him literally and nod, as if I too speak to buried people all the time. He is talking about, I learn, the telephone company workers who handle all the buried telephone wires. I prefer to think about "Buried People"—I see them stuck in the sandy soil of this place, trying to communicate with me, telling me that my longing is also their longing—that life may go on, but it need not evolve upward—it may simply go in circles, or in spirals: at least that is what they've seen, buried as they are.

When Mike called on Friday afternoon, I had almost given up on him. Yes, he had gotten the note. Yes, he would drive down for the party. I gave him directions to the State Capitol Building in Santa Fe, and told him I would meet him there the next afternoon.

"Hey, I couldn't find you yesterday morning," I said, not wanting to end the phone conversation.

After a beat, he replied, "I was hiding." I kept my ear to the phone: was there going to be more? Was he hiding from me? If not me, who or what had caused him to disappear into the ethers?

"I see. Well, I'm glad you came out of hiding… I mean, here you are." We both hung on for a few moments, I enjoying the simple feeling of connection and sensing that he was getting equal pleasure from it.

"See you tomorrow," he said with a light laugh, ending the call.

I had not lost him. Mike had not been a dream. He called me and he was coming to see me. This time maybe someone would walk into my life and stay, I thought. Maybe it would be Mike.

The next afternoon, a few minutes before we had arranged to meet, I pulled into the parking lot across from the Capitol and was surprised to see Mike standing next to his car, an old blue Honda that appeared to be approaching retirement age.

"I thought I'd start out early in case I got lost," he said.

"And I started out early so I could flag you down if you missed the spot." We drove to the house, then we went back downtown to shop for some things we needed for the party that evening. On the way back home I asked Mike if he was hungry. He was, and wanted to stop at Baja Tacos, a mom-and-pop Mexican place he remembered from his teen years.

Mike was born in Albuquerque in 1973, but his family moved from there to several other cities as his father fulfilled military assignments. Later, the family moved back to New Mexico, this time to Santa Fe, for four years. Here during his middle-school years, he became familiar with the town, particularly the teenage hangouts.

We got back to the house a little after three in the afternoon. The party would not begin until around seven. All the time we were together shopping and snacking, my sexual energy was mounting. I was looking forward to this time alone for the same kind of gentle lovemaking we had had a few short nights before. I assumed Mike was in the same mood. But when we stretched out on the bed and I moved to touch him, he patted my hand and said he felt really tired and would like to take a nap.

My first thought was that I had lost him again, this time for good. He might be interested in men, but not in me—as a lover, at least. I lay there beside him while he drifted effortlessly into a light sleep. Half an hour later, unable to relax, I got up and went to the kitchen to chop vegetables. My high spirits of earlier in the day plummeted as I worked at the chopping block. My eyes welled up with tears that might have been coming from the onions, but surely were also from frustration and dashed hopes.

During the party I felt myself divided between being an upbeat host and a disappointed suitor. Every time I looked at Mike my heart sank. As I watched him chatting quietly with my friends, munching on potato salad, laughing softly, I tried to imagine a life with him. That would not happen, of course, because, in spite of our passionate one-night encounter, it was clear he was not interested in me in that way. I smiled bravely as he came toward me.

"Joseph, I have to go," he said over the music. "I should have told you before…I have a massage client in the morning, so I need to take off now." Then, maybe because he saw my smile suddenly fade, he added, "Great party."

I kissed him on the cheek and watched him weave around clusters of partygoers to the door. And then, again, he was gone.

Could it be that all I see in you is my own self as young, the part of me I veiled with black robes and shut away in religion so no one could know my secret? I have thought of that—searching all my life through for the boy who was lost, hoping to recover him between the legs of young men I cared nothing for, but who gave themselves willingly to my advances for favors of one kind or another from me. Maybe you are the fugitive innocent within me, waiting to be caught, waiting to be held in the arms of a man, myself grown old, to be adored with kisses.

"I'm calling you from the University," Mike said on the phone Monday afternoon. "I'm in the Behavioral Science Building. I think it's the only place on campus where you can sit down while you're talking."

"It's good to hear from you," I said, not knowing exactly where to take the conversation. We traded small-talk about the party and the new people he had met at my place, about a hike into the mountains he had taken the day before. Then, after an awkward silence, he cleared his throat.

"Are you going to come up to Las Vegas this week?" I could tell by the slight strain in his voice that saying the words was difficult for him.

"I hadn't thought about it," I said.

"Well, if you come up, you can...you can stay with me...I mean, if you want." On the other end of the phone he waited for me to say something. If he could have seen me holding tightly onto the receiver, hardly breathing, suddenly washed over with a far-off memory, an insinuation tripped by something in his voice, his words…Was this mere *déjà vu* or were we tapping into a deeper place, the two of us, unwitting and yet knowing in some way? Was this a connection or a re-connection?

When I arrived in Las Vegas late Wednesday afternoon, one week exactly after we had first met, I went directly to Mike's house. This was the first time I saw his place, a converted porch of a small old Victorian wood-frame house. I was struck by how neatly he kept it. On the floor, he had made up his futon with what looked like fresh sheets and a brown wool blanket. Mike, with his long hair pulled back, dressed in clean Levis and a dark red shirt with a proper collar, appeared neat, as well. The thought that this might be a "date" had not occurred to me, but here it was.

We headed out to a diner on Bridge Street for a sandwich. I found it easy to talk to him, and found, to my surprise, that there seemed to be a lot to talk about. Walking back to the house, I brushed up to him and briefly squeezed his hand. He held my hand for a moment and then, as a car rolled by, he dropped it.

At the house, we sipped red wine and he lighted some candles that were scattered around the room on a bookcase, a night-table, a window ledge. He put a cassette tape into his little stereo—something contemporary, bouncy but soft, and unrecognizable to me, for which he apologized—and invited me to sit on the futon.

My passion for him, his beautiful dancer's body and his gentle manner, mixed with the tremendous gratitude I felt for his acceptance and his willingness to bring me into his life. I set my wine glass down and kissed him, and then we were in each other's arms for hours into the late summer night. We drifted off to sleep, and then just before dawn we made love again. I held him close and tight, as if he might disappear if I did not. He sighed and rested his head on my shoulder, a hand on my chest over my heart.

Later, when we were up and about and he had brought us coffee from the kitchen, I told him how I had been feeling over the weekend, as if he was not interested in me, and how disappointed I had been.

"Yeah, I thought you might have been a little confused at how I was behaving," he said as we made up the futon. "I guess I had to sort out my own feelings. This has all been pretty fast."

"Maybe I'm feeling that at my age faster is better," I said with a chuckle. We took opposite ends of a sheet and folded it together.

"You're not old," he said, suddenly serious. "Besides, I like guys who are more…mature."

"That's interesting. I've always been attracted to younger men, like you." I stacked the folded sheets on the edge of the futon, then leaned over and kissed him. "Don't you find guys your age attractive?"

"Not really. They don't have any lines on their faces," he said, tracing his fingers over my brow. "Their faces don't have, you know, character. If you want to know the truth, with guys my age, sometimes I can't even tell them apart."

Chapter Four

We walked down to Bridge Street for breakfast, then ambled back in the mid-morning August heat to his house, talking and joking all the way. At the house I kissed him good-bye, got into my car, and drove back to Santa Fe. Mike said he would call me about coming to visit me on Saturday. He did call and he did come to Santa Fe, and that started a long-distance courtship—he coming to see me on the weekend, me going to see him on Wednesday—that would continue through the next four months.

Chapter Five

I had dismissed the idea of a religious vocation all through my school years until, as a senior in high school, I went to a career-night and heard a Brother of Holy Cross give a talk. Brothers were professional religious men, he explained, the group was a teaching order, the life was monastic—based on the practice of the vows of Poverty, Chastity, and Obedience. At once, I knew this was for me. A week after graduation, the parish priest himself drove me to Watertown, Wisconsin, where the Brothers of Holy Cross received their Postulants.

My decision seemed impetuous, but I suppose the notion had been inside me for a very long time. I suppose it was the same impulse that had drawn me as a child to collect holy cards, to enjoy the pageantry of the Our Lady of Mt. Carmel Feasts and the Corpus Christi processions with the priest in gold vestments under a canopy carried by four men and the melodrama of Solemn High Masses—and to serve for several years as an altar boy. It might have started with seeing a string of black wooden rosary beads twined around the post of my grandmother's bed, a votive candle flickering on a picture of the Sacred Heart of Mary in my aunt's parlor. It must have begun when I felt that surge of erotic energy when Robbie and I performed our naked sacred rituals in the tool shed.

For years afterward I would look for the reasons why, at the age of seventeen, I would want to seal myself off in a monastery. Everyone around me was beginning life at that time; I appeared to be ending my life. At the high school graduation ceremony, the speeches were about starting out into the world; but I was retreating from the world, going into hiding behind monastery walls. A week to the day after that ceremony, I would leave home forever to enter a life of self-denial, celibacy, and silence.

For one who was about to give up "the world," I was not the least bit worldly. My experience with life up to that time was rather limited. Sexually, I was an innocent. Two make-out sessions with girls during high school, one at an Explorer Scout party, the other after a sock-hop, had led to nothing more than blue-balls. I had not done anything with a boy, either, though the thought was intriguing. An older neighbor boy had a stack of *Confidential* magazines by his bedside. I found them one day, looked at an article called "Homos—They May Be in Your Town!" and broke out in a sweat.

I had no way of knowing at that time where my decision to become a monk would take me. In school we had learned a little about the lives of monks in the Middle Ages, not much about modern monastic life. But I do remember that once I made the decision, a great feeling of peace came over me. It just seemed right.

When I entered the monastery, the reason I gave to others, and to myself, was to serve God. If pressed, I wouldn't have known what that meant, exactly. The real reason, I understood, was to isolate and insulate myself from the world: to hide. That much I knew; I did not yet know what I felt I needed to hide *from*. Over the next eight years behind the walls, I would discover why I had a burning desire to quit the world at an early age and commit to spending the rest of my life in silence and solitude.

Along the way I would experience a profound loneliness, painful enough to cast a shadow over all the rest of my life. I also would glimpse the ecstasy that is written about in spiritual literature—the indescribable thrill of being ablaze with divine love, and of being loved divinely in return. I was aroused and transported by the passionate sexual implications in the words of consecration uttered over the little round white host at Mass—"This is my body...eat of it."

To be sure, there was more loneliness than ecstasy behind the walls. In that darkness, not even those brief moments of rapture could cancel out the heart-aching emptiness of isolation, it seemed. Then the feeling would come again, a shiver like a quick grace, and I would be able to tolerate another day or another hour.

Still, paradoxically, I loved the loneliness. If it was painful beyond words, it was also somehow appropriate for what I was doing. I loved the isolation of the monastery much more than the religious trappings that filled it. Christian monasticism is tied to religious practice, but the essence of the monastic life is not necessarily the practice of religion. The life of the monk is a life apart from the world—whether it is the medieval world of warring feudal lords and social chaos or the modern world of materialism, greed, and moral chaos. What appealed most to me in living a monastic life was not the perfect practice of religion, but the experience of hermitage. I wanted to get away from the world I knew and bury myself in another place, in another time.

I wanted, finally I understood, to hide from my sexuality.

೦⁄೨

The God I knew as a monk was still the God of my childhood—a man, decidedly, a wise old man. Everything around me supported this fantasy, from the reproductions of old masters in prayer books to the ornate fittings of the chapel. In my mind, God was in a place. God reigned like a king, and if I stayed on my path and did not stray too much, I would join Him in the paradise that He created moment to moment with the light of His divine power. I could never get above the idea that the heaven toward which I was apparently traveling might be terribly boring; I could not get my head around the notion of eternity as more than time going on and on and on—but the alternative was too frightening to entertain.

Later I would come to realize that my entire spiritual journey would be one of trying to know what God is—what It is, how It operated in the world, and what my response to It should be. But at the time I lived a medieval monastic life, worshipping a medieval God, enthroned in splendor in the chapel of the monastery. I understood this notion of the divinity perfectly. It was theatrical and emotion provoking. The Christmas I spent in the novitiate—the first year of being a monk, a year of silence—was such a theatrical event that I can remember every moment of it even now, fifty years later. Midnight Mass, Latin chant, candles, incense, the first Mass at dawn, the choir intoning *Christus natus est*—"the Christ is born." I was in a state of rapture. I could understand how the saints could be lifted off the ground in the sight of such a heart-opening display.

I would see over the years that I have spent my entire life till now trying to frame a picture of God, and trying not to. That is, I have been formulating mostly through the process of elimination, a God that I find sensible and correct to me. And so the arc of my life out of religion and into spirituality is in essence the journey from the God of my childhood toward the God of my adulthood. I wonder if this is not the story of our species in miniature and somehow personalized. It is the image of God—something to pray to, something to worship—that I have been seeking. It is the face of God I have been looking for.

In the monastery, there are no mirrors. Odd that of the thousands of memories I have of monastic life, this one should visit me so often. Often when I pass a mirror now or look into one, I remember that for so long I was not able to see myself. We had a very small mirror in our cells, but this, no larger than the palm of the hand, was to shave by. Even then, we were warned against peering too closely at ourselves, to exercise the custody of the eyes in the mirror.

Whether the lack of mirrors was about vanity or something else, I never grasped. Was it to cultivate a spiritual understanding of oneself by negating the physical? What happens in a world without mirrors is that we don't know what we look like in the flesh, and so we begin to have a concept of ourselves as almost disembodied. It is the denial of the flesh in order to emphasize the spirit. It was part of the medieval religious scenario, where the flesh was bad and spirit good, and we are living in a dualistic universe where good will—must—triumph against evil in the end.

After I left the monastery I rented an apartment that had an old-fashioned beveled full-length mirror attached to the closet door. I remember gazing into it, being mesmerized by my reflection, and aroused. I admired my body, and understood in a flash of insight how this act of seeing oneself in glass would go against every philosophy in monastic life—and would, if given into, topple it. I supposed the idea was to give as little attention as possible to the body in order to keep the mind focused on the things of the spirit.

I know now, of course, that the matters of the body and the spirit are one, and to deny any part of that unity is to deny all of it. Still, the sight of myself in the flower of my young manhood was incontestably stimulating, and, behind the walls, would have steered me down forbidden sexual paths. Arousal would not have been enough; masturbation would not have been enough: I would have wanted to seek partners, to seek groups.

I see that I entered the monastery with a pure heart to seek God. But what I found was an amplified version of the God of my childhood religion. I gave myself to that God for eight years—in silence, in contemplation, in prayers, in good works—and knew, finally, that this God was not enough, was not the true God. There must be a God behind and above this one that is the God I wanted to adore and love.

Nevertheless I pronounced, after seven years of practicing them, the vows of poverty, chastity, and obedience in perpetuity—perpetual vows—that would make me a monk forever. I made my vows to God not to the church that houses Him. I made them in the presence of the saints and martyrs of the faith, in the sight of the Mother of God, and in the company of my brothers. I made them in full view of my family, as witnesses. I made my vows to God—the God of my childhood and the God of the medieval monastery. A year later I walked away from all of it.

I lived only one year under perpetual vows. It was one of the worst years of my life, because all during it I was drawn to life on the outside, and knew that I could never have that now. What pulled me was the vigor of my youth, the excitement of making an impact, the sheer fun of the outside.

The summer after I pronounced final vows I spent in a house in the Midwest with not many duties. I often left the house and went walking. The sight of people intoxicated me. I was heartbroken that I had separated myself from them perpetually. One day I was in the parlor of the house reading a newsmagazine—for now, in the mission houses, these were allowed. The magazine carried an article about rebelling youth, the emergence of a generation of young people that was flaunting authority and taking their lives into their own hands. The pictures that accompanied the article were of young men and women, my age and younger, wearing colorful clothes and painting their bodies. The boys had long, bushy golden hair and were stripped to the waist; the girls wore strands of beads and some of them bared their breasts. It was incredibly stimulating to me.

That year I had been sent to study. In the university I began to encounter more and more people my age who were emerging as a powerful voice, and who were finding their own voice. They were having fun.

Over that year, and probably before, I had begun to entertain the idea that God is in the world. This ran counter to the life I was leading, and to which I had given myself body and soul. For the wisdom of the monastery was that God would be found within the walls, even though it allowed that salvation could be attained in any walk of life. Life in the monastery was "the fullness of the religious life," and, as such, was the dwelling place of God.

Now I had begun to question that premise. God, suddenly, was "out there" in the world, waiting for me to find It and to embrace It.

Chapter Six

In mid-September, around the time of my fifty-sixth birthday, I received an unexpected royalty check from the European publisher of *Live Better Longer*. When I went up to Las Vegas that week I told Mike I would like to acknowledge the foreign sales of the book by spending some of the royalty money in Las Vegas because of its proximity to Sapello, where Dr. Parcells lived the last few years of her life. I had the idea to take him to the local supermarket to stock up on food and supplies.

"I don't want you to do that," he said. "Really, I don't. I can manage on my own."

"I understand—you don't want me to be a sugar-daddy to you, and believe me I don't want you to think of me that way. But I've been spending a lot of time up here with you. Maybe we could cook sometimes and not go out. And if we're going to do that, you need to have food in the house."

"Okay," he said after a long moment, "as long as you know I'm not asking you for anything." Mike was making a ground-rule for what might become a relationship. If it was to be, it would be founded on an equal sharing of resources and mutual respect. I was not to try to buy his friendship; he was not to be a "kept" boy.

We shopped that day and had enormous fun. He gravitated toward self-serve bulk items like oatmeal and rice and beans. I tossed into the cart a big bag of potato chips and a pound of sugar cookies, insisting that he treat himself from time to time. We also bought cat food for Madre, his long-haired black cat. He told me that a few weeks before he had bundled Madre in his backpack and taken her to this store. He let her out in the pet food aisle and, to the amusement of the other shoppers, allowed her to choose her own suppers and snacks.

The trunk of my car was filled with bags of groceries; we could hardly lower the trunk lid over them. We feasted that evening on grilled chicken breasts and steamed vegetables and wine, and Mike's little pantry was filled to the brim.

Over dinner he told me a story that caught my heart. A few months earlier, Mike had fallen on hard times. He had graduated from massage school—the prestigious Jay Sherer Academy in Santa Fe—and, after wandering around for a couple of years, had settled here in Las Vegas with little promise of being able to generate an income.

"This is a depressed area," he reminded me, handing me the salad bowl. "People may have a little money for food and clothing, but there is nothing left over for something like a corrective massage, even if they're in pain. To them, it's a total luxury. I started to feel sort of strapped. I didn't want to ask my folks for money, so I swallowed my pride and applied for food stamps."

"That must have been hard for you."

"Yeah it was. But up here, half the town is on stamps. I was just another unemployed person who needed help."

He easily qualified for the little government card that allowed him to have some food in the house—no soap or shampoo, no alcohol, nothing non-essential, no cat food. As if on cue, Madre jumped down off her perch on the windowsill and rubbed herself against my leg.

Two months after Mike was awarded food stamps, he was offered a job by his friend Andi, a jewelry-maker, to work in her shop as her assistant, sanding, and polishing some of her original design silver and gold pieces. He also learned from her how to design and make his own pieces.

"When I got the job, I went back to the food stamp office and turned in my card," he said as we were finishing our dinner with sugar cookies. "There were credits left on it, but I just didn't want to use them."

"You gave your stamp-credits back?"

"Well, yeah," he said, taking another tiny bite of his cookie, as if he was going to make it last the whole evening. "That is, I *tried* to give them back," he continued. "The woman said she didn't know what to do with them. She said it was the first time since she had worked there that someone had returned stamps."

"How long had she worked at the stamp office?" I asked him, caught up in the story and imagining it in my mind.

Mike shrugged. "Nineteen years, I think she said."

This morning I woke before you and watched you sleeping. Little lines are starting to show around your eyes, so thin they seem to be drawn by the fine point of a sharp pencil. You are getting older, too. This face that I have been looking at for more than a decade is maturing, ripening, cracking here and there in tiny crow's feet, creasing in the corners of your beautiful mouth.

Fall came to the Sange de Cristo Mountains as our courtship continued, growing sweeter and warmer even as the year waned. We took drives up into the mountains to see the full splendor of the golden aspens flinging their doubloon leaves in the wind like profligate conquistadores. We rode through some of the villages on the high road to Taos, stopping for lunches of fresh roasted green *chile* peppers and pinto beans cooked with pork.

༄

Thursday, December 20

When morning comes, my body feels lumpish. I pull myself out of bed. Mike is up already, packing the shaving kit that we share. I hear our tooth brushes go into the small leather bag, dental floss, shampoo, brush, then the zipper closes.

We took this huge seven-bedroom house with Beverly six months ago to be in a quiet neighborhood a few blocks from the *Jardin* and to have room for guests coming to San Miguel for retreats. Unlike the Colonials closer to the town center, with their arches, pillars, and courtyards, this is a stately three-story Mexico City style home on a small park. A generous back patio accommodates our two cars and three motor scooters. Two seating and eating areas covered by English ivy and carmine-colored bougainvilleas share the patio garden.

Christina, an artist friend, has come to pick up Mike and me and drive us to Queretaro, our nearest big urban center, about an hour away, where we will meet the bus for the Mexico City airport. I go downstairs lugging my suitcase and into the kitchen.

"You look grumpy," Christina says, sipping a coffee.

"I didn't sleep well," I mutter. "Maybe it was the *ceviche* I ate last night."

Out the car window on the way to Queretaro, the dusty scrub and cactus on the corrugated desert hills cast shadows that look like little people in the strong morning sun. I suddenly have the stinging urge to pee. I am holding it in uncomfortably until, finally, I ask Christina to pull over at the next gas station. We are on a tight schedule, but we just have to stop. At the station, the door to the bathroom has a coin-operated handle. I sort through the change in my pocket and, finding only large coins, go back to the car and get a two-peso coin from Mike. By this time, I am almost wetting my pants. At last, I relieve myself in the bathroom, waiting a few moments for the pee to start coming out.

We arrive at the bustling Queretaro bus terminal with two minutes to spare. Fortunately, we have bought tickets ahead of time. We will take one of the Mexican luxury buses, with seats as wide and comfortable as first-class airplane seats and, floating above every three rows or so, television monitors playing hit movies. On the three-hour ride to Mexico City, Mike dozes like a child, but I am restless. I get up to go to the bathroom four times. Each time, I feel somewhat relieved, but the flow out of me is slow and hesitant, and it burns a little. Mike is awake when I get back to my seat the last time.

"What's going on—are you okay?" he asks, his eyes going to my pants.

"I think I have Restless Leg Syndrome, Doctor."

"We might have to operate," he says with a wry little smile.

The Mexico City airport, one of the largest in the world, is crowded and chaotic today, five days before Christmas. The shiny chrome, glass, and marble of this place, is jarring after the soft splendors of San Miguel. Shop after shop, under garish white light, selling a repetitious round of the same high-end jewelry, watches, shoes, cell phones, sun glasses, and laptops add to the metallic hardness all around us. Fast-food counters, equally repetitive with their burgers and tacos and pizzas, are crammed full of restless, jostling travelers in various stages of coming from somewhere and going to somewhere else.

We are both disoriented for a few minutes, then we find the airline desk, check in, fill out our immigration forms, and head for the gate. It is noon and we are to leave at two o'clock—plenty of time to have lunch. Over our meal, I need to go to the men's room twice. Mike is getting concerned, I can tell. I say I am fine, but having to pee a lot. He looks at me suspiciously. In a few months he will be a naturopathic doctor, a profession toward which he has applied six years of study: my brave façade does not fool him, I think.

Two o'clock, the departure time, comes and goes. The plane will be delayed by a half hour, the loudspeaker says in Spanish. Then, after that time has expired, another announcement says the plane will be delayed an hour more. I try to make myself comfortable on the hard waiting room seats.

Every ten or fifteen minutes, now, I need to pee. Each time I go to the men's room I am careful to appear as ordinary as possible, because I am concerned that the attendant, an old man in a soiled blue jumpsuit uniform, may report me for going in there so much. In my mind, I time the flow; eleven seconds of pee. When it is more, even by a second or two, I think maybe I am getting better—that this is not so serious.

Six hours pass. Mike, observing my frequent trips to the bathroom over the paperback book he is reading, says, "You may have a urinary tract infection."

Yes, I think. There is something wrong, something simple.

"That sounds right," I say, lightening somewhat now that the ailment is real and has a label. Since the plane is so late, I decide to try to find a *farmacia* in the airport to buy an antibiotic. In Mexico, most medicines that require a prescription from a doctor in the United States are available for the asking at pharmacies manned by well-educated and trained pharmacists. All the back-and-forth to the men's room has made me tired. I hail an electric mini-transport, a people-mover, and a young man named Javier takes me to a *farmacia*, seemingly half a kilometer away. I would never have been able to walk to it and then walk back to the gate. I buy something which the white-coated young woman behind the counter assures me is an antibiotic for an *infección de tracto urinario*.

Maybe it is my imagination, but less than an hour later, still waiting for the delayed plane, which we now learn was defective and had to be repaired, I am feeling better. My pee is orange. By the time we leave for Houston, we have waited almost eight hours. In Houston, because all the flights for San Antonio have left long ago, we are bussed to a boxy, no-frills hotel a few miles from the airport. We will be picked up there at five-thirty in the morning to resume our journey; it is after midnight. Everything in the room smacks of prefab, built-in, quick-clean utility; even the cloth bedspreads have the feel of plastic — you could spill a cup of coffee on them and wipe them completely dry in a second with a paper towel. I get into one of the two beds and fall asleep instantly.

Chapter Seven

Ten Years Before

On one of the weekend evenings Mike spent with me in Santa Fe, we went out to a movie. Afterwards, sitting in the car in the driveway, our conversation drifted toward the future. I asked him what he wanted to do in the next few months and years—at twenty-five, his whole life was ahead of him.

Two or three weeks after we met, Mike had told me about his epileptic seizures, which had begun after an automobile accident — he was a passenger in the back seat — in Albuquerque when he was still in high school. For months after the accident, he had suffered full seizures from time to time until his doctor settled on a medication to lessen their frequency and maybe prevent them altogether. Now he was on an anticonvulsant medication, three little red-and-white capsules that he took every night before he went to sleep. As long as he remembered to take his pills, he was fine. If he forgot, even one night, he ran the risk of a seizure. In Las Vegas the year before we met, he forgot and had a mild seizure while driving and ran into a stop sign attempting to pull off onto the shoulder. Fortunately, he was not hurt and no other vehicles were on the road.

Sitting next to me in the car on that October night, bundled up in our fleece jackets, he said he had some difficulty seeing his future. The "disability" of the epilepsy made him think that he would never have a real career, or even hold a real job. Anything he turned his hand to might end up a disaster if he was hit with a seizure at a crucial moment.

"But you don't have seizures if you take your meds, right?" I asked him, genuinely curious.

"Right," he said.

A sudden gust of wind came up and blew a flutter of yellowish-brown cottonwood leaves scratching across the windshield. I looked past the leaves at the faint outline of the coyote fence that surrounded the house, straight spikes of gnarled old wood catching the light from the lamp in the living room window. The neighbor's white cat, making her nightly rounds, stopped and looked at us from the stoop leading into our house, then scampered away into the darkness.

"You are not defective," I said. I seemed to be hearing myself saying this, such was the force of the message—it was as if it was being channeled from some deep place outside myself. "But, look, you can do anything you want. You can be anything you want to be."

Part of me wondered where this was coming from. I had been avoiding any kind of direct mentoring because I wanted our relationship, if there was to be one, to be equal and even, not unbalanced with me as a surrogate parent and him my fantasy son. I was profoundly aware that my thirty years seniority automatically offered me control of the partnership. I desperately wanted us to be equals loving each other.

But this time, at least, something was pushing me to focus in like a good therapist on a core belief that I knew was holding Mike back from living a full, productive life and would, in time, sabotage the connection we were trying to build with each other.

Even in the shadowy light, I could see Mike's eyes glisten and shine. Now he began to sob. I reached over and put my arm around him, and he pressed himself onto my chest.

"They told me…they told me…" His voice trailed off as he wiped his tears away.

"Someone told you that you were defective in some way?"

He nodded. "When I was in the eighth-grade I overheard my grandfather tell my dad something about my brother and me—what Grandpa said was, 'These boys of yours are not too smart…you should think about putting them in some kind of trade school so they can learn a skill and get a job.' It was the first time I had thought about being smart or not-smart. I felt just awful."

A chill ran through me. Good Lord, I thought, how could someone be so cruel as to render such a harsh, definitive judgment on a child—especially with the child in the room and within earshot? Another squall of leaves spattered across the windshield, as if to seal the cold and bitter verdict of Mike's grandfather.

"What if he was wrong?" I said. "What if you are smart—not only intelligent, but strong and healthy and not flawed in any way?"

Mike looked deep into my eyes and it was almost as if he was processing new information, asking me if what I said could possibly be true.

"Because that's how I see you," I said. "Everything I see in you is exactly right...you are exactly right, just the way you are. I'm a picky Virgo —do you think I could fall in love with anyone who wasn't perfect?"

We both laughed softly. He rolled in closer and I gathered him to me with both arms. "I love you," he said.

"And I love you, my Mike."

The next morning, as we were dressing for the day, I suddenly stopped, seated on the bed ready to tie my shoes, and looked at him.

"Don't hurt me," I said. I held my shoelaces in my hand. It was as if time had stopped and I had stumbled upon a core belief of my own—one that apparently had prevented me from entering a meaningful relation with anyone for years, all my life, really: a fear of being hurt.

"What? What do you mean?" From the tone of his voice I could tell that he may have thought I was accusing him of harming me in some way.

"Just please don't ever hurt me, okay?" My request was followed by a sudden flood of emotion that swept through me, and just as quickly was gone. I tied my shoes.

"Joseph, I will never hurt you." He came over to me and kissed me on the forehead.

"And I'll never hurt you, Mike." To this day, I still do not know why I said that, or why I felt I needed to say it then, but it seemed important to me at the time. Maybe I was in one quick instant identifying the one obstacle that always had prevented me from loving another and accepting another's love, and dispatching it at the same time, clearing the way for this relationship to truly bud and bloom.

I dream about death. Not death, really, but the time between now and death, so little time. In the early morning, before light begins to bleed through the drapes of white manta on our windows turning the room to gray tones where objects are barely perceptible, I lie there next to you and listen to you breathe.

I forget how old I am, and then I remember with a sinking feeling that turns to alarm. Lying here still as a corpse, my mind wanders through memories of our brief time together. How much is left of this? How will I be in five years? In ten, should I survive?

Our lovemaking was tender and sweet, at times ravenous, as if we had been starved for sensual touch for so long and had been denied it. For me, it had been years since I had been entwined in the arms of someone who was not a stranger. There was about these times, for me and for Mike as well, the excitement of having our deepest longings fulfilled, against the "norms" of conventional sex and love—first we were two men expressing ourselves freely and fully, second we were older man and younger man, for each of us a perfect match.

All during my eight years in monastic life, I kept my vow of chastity. Though there was temptation everywhere, it sometimes seemed, I remained celibate. Call it the grace-of-state. Somehow, I was spared the involvements that have so plagued the haunts of holy men for centuries, up to our own day. In my monastery sixty men lived under the same roof; no one ever touched a hand to me...or me to any of them.

About a year after I had left the monastery, I experienced an intense out-of-body experience. At the time, the pain of loneliness and guilt I was feeling was almost unbearable. That pain abated a little every day, as if the farther I traveled from the monastery in time, the more the pain diminished, and the easier it became to carry that burden. But still the burden was heavy.

I was in an open field atop a small hill overlooking the town. I had been walking that afternoon, and had come across this pleasant site. For once, I was not looking for sex or feeling driven by other demons. I sat down to rest under a tree. Then, after awhile, I moved to an open spot and lay down, looking up at the clouds and the gathering twilight. I closed my eyes. Within a few seconds I was up in the air looking down at myself. I could see my closed eyes, my composed face, my hands folded over my abdomen. I could see myself, but not as in a mirror, where everything is reversed. I saw myself as I am seen by others—from outside myself. This was an amazing feeling that I had never felt before. In eight years of daily meditation—an hour in the morning and an hour at night—I had not experienced anything remotely like this. I struggled to keep my eyes closed. I had wanted to check to see where I really was—up in the air hovering over my body—in my body, imagining I was floating above myself.

With my eyes still closed, I felt my penis enlarging. From where I was hovering I looked at my body, inspected it, and saw my erection. From there I roamed around the open field. I went up into trees, all the way to the top, and looked down from there. I saw picnickers leaving, a couple folding up the blanket they had been lying on. I saw a path I had not known was there before. In that fading light, the green of the grass and the tree leaves was intense and vibrant, the air was sweet. I was disembodied, but I also had senses. I went to my body again, hovered above it, checked to see if I was breathing—for I was motionless, except for a slight, almost indiscernible rise and fall of my chest. I was breathing. I saw myself take in a deep breath, and felt a great rush of air fill me. It was exquisite.

I seemed to drift off to sleep for a few minutes. Then, when I opened my eyes—the real eyes of my real body—I was staring up at a sky full of starlight.

Anyone could argue that a man in such a state as I was at the time—confused, caught between two worlds—could have what might seem like an out-of-body experience, but might simply be experiencing the symptoms of stress. But I know what I felt and saw that night, and it has remained with me as the first step out of religious experience into spiritual experience. When I was in the monastery, I had read of the ecstasy of saints—how some of them would levitate in meditation, for instance. This was like that. It was the perfect knowledge of oneness with everything in the universe, and the feeling that I was a spirit, and capable of going anywhere, even up to those stars, and doing anything. I was free of my body. I was not my body.

To live as a spiritual being in a spiritual universe is to have that knowledge. I was grateful for that experience. It changed me. It started me thinking that I might have left the comforts and confines of the monastery for a good reason: to explore a personal spirituality that went beyond religion. It allowed me to entertain the possibility that I had closed the door and walked away from sacred vows in the religion of my childhood so that I could begin to enter higher mysteries. I took the episode in the meadow as a confirmation of my sincere desire to continue my journey in the realm of the spirit. It was an opening onto that spiritual plane that had eluded me inside the walls.

Chapter Eight

Friday, December 21

Miraculously, I have had to get up in the night to pee only twice. Mike answers the hotel wake-up call at five-fifteen, then gets out of his bed and lays down next to me on my bed and kisses me on the cheek—in ten years, we can count the few nights we have slept apart. For a few precious moments, we cuddle, and it is an enormous comfort to me. But now the shuttle arrives and we have to get up and leave. On the plane finally headed for San Antonio, I sit at the back, near the restroom. My pee is bright orange, reddish, mandarin and it still stings on the way out. When Mike asks me to describe what I am feeling, I resist the temptation to tell him that it is like passing razor blades to pee. I just shrug and brave a little smile.

Mike's father, Bill, meets us an hour and a half later at the San Antonio airport's baggage claim.

He is around sixty, on the stout side, ruddy-faced, with wired-rimmed bifocals half-way down his nose, making him look slightly Pickwickian. He is career military, a lawyer, now a judge who decides disability cases. Their home is in a gated community on San Antonio's upper middle class North Side, a comfortable new place in a development of big look-alike homes that Sharron, Mike's mother, has filled with framed photos and knick-knacks she has been carrying from place to place over the many years of Bill's military obligations. Sharron is three years younger than her husband, to whom she has been married for thirty-six years, auburn-haired, cheerful, motherly. Sharron has put up a huge Christmas tree loaded with tasteful ornaments in one corner of the living room, displacing a couch and an end table, which are now rearranged next to two overstuffed leather recliners facing a monster television screen; their recliners may as well have their names on them.

The house smells of butter and cookies: Sharron has been making several different varieties of peanut brittle as gifts for the neighbors. Both Mike and I are zombies from rising so early and from the delays of the day before, so we excuse ourselves and go to bed in the guestroom. I am warm with a fever. Three hours later, waking up groggily, we both have the urge to make love. In spite of my painful peeing through the day, my ejaculation is pleasant and normal. Is this, whatever it is, passing through? Am I getting better?

When we rejoin the parents in the living room in the early afternoon, the talk is of shopping and presents. I tell Sharron how I have been feeling. Behind her sympathetic eyes I can see her mental gears working; she had been, some years before, a respiratory therapist. She and Mike decide that we all should go shopping at a nearby mall. When I say I want to go back to bed, Sharron tells me gently that I should think about seeing a doctor.

"It just doesn't sound good," she says.

༄

Ten Years Before

Once, when we were getting into bed, I heard Mike whispering excitedly to himself, "Yes! Yes!"

"What are you going on about?" I asked him.

"I asked the Universe to give me a boyfriend who wasn't a creep. I'm just saying thank-you. Yes! My boyfriend *is not a creep!*" We teased each other and giggled so loudly that we thought we might wake up the house.

A few days before Thanksgiving, my housemates announced they were moving to Washington, D.C., where a new job awaited. It seemed natural that Mike, who was spending more and more time at the house in Santa Fe, would move down from Las Vegas and come to live with me.

I helped him pack up his things in the little apartment that had been the scene of our first full flowering of passion. Among his belongings was a small box of jewelry-making tools, some of which he had bought for himself and others that Andi, his boss and teacher, had given to him.

"What's this?" I asked, pulling a tiny manila envelope out of the box.

"It's left-over gold and silver from one of Andi's projects. She gave it to me. She said someday maybe I'll use it for one of my own pieces."

With more room in the house than we could use, we advertised for another housemate. Diane, a pert and savvy blonde in her forties answered the ad. She had moved to Santa Fe two years earlier from New York and had begun a photography darkroom business. In this city of artists, the Darkroom, as she also called her business, nestled in alongside picture framers and art supply shops, promised to be a successful venture. Mike moved into the house the first week of December; Diane moved in a week later.

Two weeks before Christmas, just as we were getting settled in together, Mike's parents, who were living in Minneapolis, announced out of the blue that they were going to be visiting us in Santa Fe, and indeed were on their way. It was the only time I ever remember pacing the floor. I actually walked back and forth across the bedroom floor, back and forth, as if I was madly measuring the room and coming up with frustratingly false readings.

"Do you realize you are pacing?" Mike said, amused. "You're making me nervous."

"Well, your parents are coming." I continued to pace the floor, but slower and more deliberately. And I noticed that I was—unbelievably—wringing my hands, as if I was washing them with air.

"They're going to like you, I'm sure."

"Maybe, but do they know...do they know my age?" I asked him, my voice rising uncontrollably. I walked over to Mike and grabbed him by the shoulders. "I mean, your dad is a career military man and a lawyer—they could sue me or something, maybe have me thrown in jail."

"In jail! For what?" Mike laughed. "Relax—I told them all about you, and they seem fine with our being together." He sat on the edge of the bed and patted the mattress, inviting me to sit next to him. I did, trying to calm myself. But I was not successful.

"Did you tell them my age?" I asked him again, momentarily imagining a scene of operatic proportions, with accusations flying and tears flowing.

"They know I like older men. I told them...let's see...I actually told them that the three of you would probably have a lot in common."

"Good Lord!" I said, jumping up off the bed and picking up my pacing.

I had always been private about my sexuality. All during my more than twenty years in Santa Fe, I was careful to present myself either as vaguely heterosexual or as a sexual question-mark. I had several women friends, two or three in particular who accompanied me to social functions. I was particularly careful, or tried to be, during the time I was a college professor. In the wake of Anita Hill, who made sexual harassment famous during the Clarence Thomas Supreme Court hearings, and the priest-pedophiles scandals—my college had originated as a Catholic institution—it seemed prudent to fly under the radar, as they say.

Running parallel to this reticence to reveal myself had been the nagging issue of which sex I really was attracted to. I enjoyed the company of women immensely and appreciated their beauty and grace. But I was clearly more attracted to men as objects of sexual desire. For years I sat, increasingly uncomfortably, on a fence between two preferences.

With the parental visit looming, I was about to finally declare myself. And that was frightening beyond words.

The next day Bill and Sharron called from their hotel, got directions to the house from Mike, and half an hour later arrived at our front door. By then I had calmed down enough to be cordial and composed. Somewhere in the back of my mind a drama was running in which Bill, like the elder Germont in *La Traviata*, would take me aside and try to reason with me, explaining how continuing this relationship with his young son would ruin his life and bring shame upon the family. Or Sharron, gasping my hand tightly, would implore me to think not about myself, but the boy, who surely needed to be free to pursue a partnership with someone more his own...age.

We are oddities, you and I. We are the subjects of psychological studies called "Age Disparity in Sexual Relationships." There is a rule of social acceptability—you were not aware of that, were you? The rule is half-your-age-plus-seven. That is what is acceptable. When I met you, I was fifty-five years old. Half that is twenty-seven and six months. Half that plus seven is thirty-four and six months.

But you were only twenty-five—almost ten years younger than you should have been for us to be acceptable.

Maybe we should have known about this rule before we fell in love with each other—I with the supple beauty of your youth, you with the dignified bearing of my age.

But since you were younger than half-my-age-plus-seven when we met, we may fall into other psychological categories. For instance, there is Chronophilia, the term for any age-related preference outside our age group. There is Ephebophilia, the attraction of older people to adolescents. Pedophilia does not apply because you were past preadolescence when we met. But there is Gerontophilia, the attraction of non-elderly people to the elderly. I believe we may qualify there, certainly.

We also come under the general heading of Paraphilia, which is when individuals exclusively pursue age-disparate relationships to the exclusion of more appropriate ones. Their behavior, classified as Parasexual, is considered "a departure from the norm."

Surely all this has passed through the thoughts of your parents as they approach me. Surely their disappointment will show on their faces and they turn away from me.

But, to my surprise, none of those scenes materialized. Instead, Bill and Sharron were friendly, engaging, and, as far as I could tell, fully accepting. As Mike had suggested, we did have many things in common. Besides being members of the same generation, on the leading edge of the boomer age bracket, all three of us were children of the 1950s, with all the common references that implies. They both had been brought up Catholic and had raised their two sons as Catholics, another important point of contact among the three of us. Bill, brainy and rather intense at our first meeting, talked almost non-stop. Later, Mike laughed about it and said his dad talks a lot when he is nervous.

Later that afternoon we took the parents shopping at a bookstore in downtown Santa Fe. Over a cup of hot chocolate in the bookstore's café, Sharron and I tried to exchange as much personal information as we could in the short time of their visit.

When there was a break in the conversation, Sharron said, "I want you to know that we are fine with this." She picked up a last bite of her croissant, but instead of eating it, put it daintily back on its plate. "I mean you and Mike. Bill and I are glad he's found someone."

"Thanks, that means a lot to me," I said sincerely—and with an audible sigh of relief. I gulped back the rest of my hot chocolate, searching around for something else to say.

But Sharron had more to tell me. "There is something you need to know about Mike. Some people are givers and some are takers. Mike is not a taker." Her eyes suddenly welled with tears.

"You've obviously done a good job parenting him," I said, taking her hand in mine and patting it gently.

"I hope so. But that quality in Mike I'm telling you about—not taking advantage of people or circumstances—is all his. He's been that way since he was a little boy."

Chapter Eight

I could almost see Mike's childhood pass across the screen of her face: Mike running into the house to greet her after school, holding up a crayon drawing he had made of her; Mike taking a first unsteady ride on a bicycle as she watched anxiously from the driveway; Mike sitting on a stool in the kitchen as she trimmed his hair and pasted it up into a Mohawk.

After Mike's parents left town, something seemed to shift for me—and for Mike, as well, I think. We became closer and even more relaxed with each other. Something significant had transpired during their visit. On the most visible and obvious level, we had all met, they had seen me and gotten to know me somewhat, they could return home assured that I was not some crazy pederast or a queer Lothario taking their son for a ride only to break his heart. I had entered their lives and they had entered mine.

Another result of the visit for me was a feeling of acceptance for exactly who and what I am. I had put myself out there as the homosexual lover of a young man, their son, and they had treated me and the situation as perfectly normal.

That atmosphere of acceptance filled the house for days afterward like the aroma of bread baking. By Christmas, we were a new family—Diane and her white spaniel, Alex; Mike and his black cat, Madre; me and my shy calico cat, Ki.

Chapter Nine

Let me tell you this as I fondle your neck and stroke your shoulder, sitting here next to you on the beach at night, watching the stars and listening to the vast Pacific Ocean pounding against the rocks of Troncones. Let me tell you all about my life before you came into it—all those years, all those loves and near-loves, the heartaches and heartbreaks, triumphs and disasters, connections and missed opportunities. By the time you were born I had already gone all through school and graduate school and had embarked on a career and had experienced love with probably two dozen men and a dozen women, some of whose faces and bodies I can remember, others not. Those were the days of easy love, of good weed and Quaaludes and a little coke and long, long Saturday afternoons.

When you were fourteen and in middle-school in Santa Fe I was teaching at a private high school not more than a mile away. I had turned forty-five and was living with a lover, a young man from a big Hispanic family. Did my path cross yours? Were we walking across the Plaza one Sunday afternoon, me going in one direction alone, you in the other direction with your brother or your buddies? Did our eyes meet briefly? Were you standing next to me watching Zozobra—Old Man Gloom—the giant piñata, go up in flames at the start of the city-wide Santa Fe Fiesta in September? Did you move in front of me to get a better look, touching my arm—this arm that I am caressing now—as you squeezed yourself through the crowd? Or did we pass each other in a grocery store aisle, coming out of a movie theater, walking into a fast-food restaurant? Waiting for a light to turn, did I catch a glimpse of you briefly looking at me from the back window of a car? Did our eyes meet for a fleeting moment?

༄

Saturday, December 22

Three days before Christmas. Mike goes out shopping again with his mother, this time to another mall across town, but I stay back at the house, too tired and peeing too frequently to go out. The antibiotic pills I bought in the Mexico City airport seem to be working, but just a bit. It is still difficult for me to make pee, and the urge to go is insistent. My penis aches. The pee is an ugly orange; it stains the toilet bowl, which I have to clean with a soiled washcloth after about every third time I go.

I am finding it difficult to get above my fears. What if this is really serious? Christmas is coming, but I am feeling far from festive. Mike and Sharron pull up in the driveway. When I hear them coming in, I get up from the bed and pretend I am puttering, wrapping presents. I do not want Mike to catch me being sick or even resting. We both know, without having spoken seriously about it, that someday I will start to decline, that I will be ill or injured or just old and tired, and he will need to take care of me, but I will put that day off as long as possible. That day is not now. Today I will be my youthful and energetic self, his equal in stamina and strength. This is the game I play.

But I am not fooling him. When we are alone, he says, "We probably should do something about this. Let's call Marc tomorrow and get some advice." Dr. Marc Walsh is a doctor friend of ours in Dallas.

"Yes, alright," I say. Then, melting into his arms, I tell him, "I'm so sorry this is happening. I'm so sorry."

Mike comforts me and, no doubt knowing I was resting when he came home, pretends to be tired and suggests we take a nap together.

༄

Nine Years Before

That winter I finished work on a new book, *The Way of the Traveler.* John Muir Publishers, a small press headquartered in Santa Fe and dedicated mainly to travel, had commissioned me to write it to launch their new body-mind-spirit line. It was to be a book about travel, but with a "spiritual" slant. Since Mike was so much a part of my life during those months, it seemed natural to dedicate the book to him.

I found during the writing that I needed to budget my time more closely than before because I wanted to spend time with Mike. The issue of attending to work, in my case forever working on a book, and taking afternoons or even whole days off to nurture our relationship has arisen many times over the years. Just when I appear to have solved the time-allotment problem, a writing deadline comes up or, on the other side, a pressing concern arises with Mike that requires me to spend more time with him, and the issue is back again. But surely every relationship has aspects of this see-saw between two poles of life demanding equal time and energy. As we lived through these together, we began to joke about them. That itself helped to defuse a potential flare-up.

One afternoon in spring Mike and I drove up to St. John's College campus and walked around the track. Only a few exercisers were out that day, jogging on the fine red cinder path and doing their stretches on the grassy inside of the giant oval. The air was fresh and bracing, snow still frosted the highest of the peaks that formed the College's imposing backdrop. As we walked, we talked about the future.

"I've always wanted to operate a retreat center," I said. "A place where people could come and be away from the world—to think, to reflect, to be quiet. I guess it's the monk in me."

"That sounds really good to me. Naturally, we would include massage and body work," Mike said with a wink.

The more we talked about the idea, the more excited we got about it. On weekends we drove out to remote areas around Santa Fe looking for a location for our retreat center. Neither of us had money to actually buy a place, but we were planning and dreaming—and we were doing it together as a joint project. We even came up with a schedule of activities at our imaginary retreat center, involving some of our friends—my friends who were quickly becoming Mike's friends: yoga instructors, astrologers, writers, spiritual teachers, artists.

For many years after leaving monastic life, I had given up religion entirely. But my interest in spirituality never flagged. I read a great deal about Buddhism and even did some study at a Zen center. Judaism always intrigued me, mainly because my strong Christian background was so rooted in it; in Santa Fe, I had a number of Jewish friends who took me with them to High Holy Days observances and Passover Seders. I also felt drawn to the philosophies of the New Age and read widely in that emerging genre of spiritual writings. Santa Fe in those days was, as it is today, a Mecca for spiritual types. I attended workshops and classes, experienced "faith-healing" from a Filipino shaman, fasted, stood long hours watching mesmeric Indian dances at the pueblos, went on guided LSD trips, did a fire-walk, joined meditation groups and spiritual discussion groups. Toward the end of my time in Santa Fe, I began a spiritual writers group. Now, with Mike, this dream of mine seemed—at least in our minds—to be coming together.

Sunday, December 23

Marc Walsh, MD, is a sandy-haired, youthful looking GP with a popular practice in Dallas. Over the past seven years, he and his wife, Barbara, a Yoga instructor, have traveled to San Miguel three times to do LifePath retreats with us. Mike and I have stayed in their home. They are like family to us.

On the phone, Marc complains about having to be on duty at the hospital during the holidays. He would rather be at home watching the basketball game with Barbara. After these preliminaries, he turns his attention to me—it is his way, his easy bedside manner. "You can wait another day and see if the Mexican antibiotics are going to work," he says after he hears my symptoms. "Then, if you're not feeling any better, get yourself to a clinic there in San Antonio and see a doc. It could be something serious."

"Serious? Like what?" I ask. I feel my stomach rising up almost to my throat.

"It might be just a bacterial infection—but it could be a prostate problem, Joseph. Could be prostate cancer."

Cancer. For the first time, I hear the name I had not allowed myself to consider. But now it has a name and, instantly, a kind of reality.

Chapter Nine

Nine Years Before

I have always had questions about what the term "soul-mate" means, but during those long spring afternoons, walking side-by-side and talking about our deepest longings and hopes for our lives, I began to think of Mike as the mate of my soul, the young man I had dreamed about but never dared to suppose would materialize. We were easy with each other, comfortable together, and content. Burdens of some sort seemed to have been lifted off both our backs.

From time to time, in the kitchen cooking together, or outdoors washing the car or cleaning up the yard, he would catch me looking at his beautiful face, his trim, limber body, and his face would open in a wide grin. I would smile back and soon we were laughing. In this way weeks passed, months.

Mike was working for a spa business started by a peppy New York transplant; she had seen an opportunity in Santa Fe's new popularity as an upscale tourist destination and grasped it by offering in-room massage services at some of the hotels around the town's historic plaza. It was an on-call job, and required him to load his portable massage table and bag of oils and creams into the trunk of his car, unload them at the hotel, lug them up and down elevators, and load them back up again in the car when he was finished. He enjoyed doing the body work, but hated the constant schlepping. And because he was working for someone else, he had to pay a hefty commission of his fee back to the owner.

"Waiters in this town are making three times as much as I am," he muttered one day after he had returned from a particularly grueling marathon involving three different locations.

A few days later he hopped into my office, which was separated from the main house by maybe fifty feet, and announced that he had quit the roving massage business and gotten a job as a waiter at a resort hotel restaurant downtown. The news melted my heart: it was a symbolic victory over what he had thought was a severe physical limitation. Mike had been worried that a permanent employment situation would end in disaster if he had a seizure on the job. By moving from being a wandering massage therapist to a nine-to-five in-place employee, he was taking a huge step forward into the territory of trust.

Nine-to-five was actually more like five-to-two. Five AM, that is. As the youngest member of a team at the restaurant he was given the early shift. His work day began at six in the morning, which meant that he needed to get up at five. I awoke with him and made coffee on his work days, trying to offer support and reinforcement for his brave and adult decision to face his demon head-on.

Mike worked on all through summer. I took a break from book-writing and got some free-lance work with Internet magazines. This was the time of the great Internet "start-ups," the first flush of websites that cropped up like mushrooms in the dark hotbed of cyberspace promoting various lifestyles, attitudes, and cultural positions. Some of the sites I worked for: Eddie Bauer.com (the clothier's chic online magazine), SharpMan.com (aimed at sophisticated urban males), Built2XL.com (for overly tall and oversized people), BeatenTrack.com (travel for life-long learners), and MyPrimeTime.com (an ambitious Baby Boomer site)—for which I was tagged an "expert" and treated with tremendous deference by a staff that played Ping-Pong and sipped cappuccinos on breaks in their vast San Francisco loft.

The idea that I could earn a living sitting in my office in Santa Fe in my underwear, providing "content" for Internet sites at the rate of a dollar a word or more, was immensely appealing to me and I threw myself into the work with great enthusiasm. In less than a year, I had earned as much as I would have with a generous book advance.

These websites offered advice and how-to information in banks of essays, but for the most part carried no advertising and included no "store" that would have generated income. Most of the start-ups shriveled up and died after they had exhausted their first bankroll from venture capitalists—who in their turn had been "investing" in these dubious enterprises without even glancing at business plans, since their intention apparently was to lose money for tax purposes. By the end of the century, few of these sites, which had been cash-cows for writers like me, survived.

In the first week of August, to celebrate the first anniversary of our meeting, Mike and I took a road trip up through Northern New Mexico and Southern Colorado, spending a few days in Purgatory (about which we made endless jokes), a ski town that in summer was devoid of snow but full of magnificent wide open mountain vistas.

We visited Durango, with its quaint Old West streets basking in the long sunny summer afternoons, and ambled past antique shops and bookstores eating ice-cream cones. We went on to Trinidad, which we learned was the sex-change capital of the country—of the world, for all we knew—and where waitresses at diners had suspiciously large hands and Adam's Apples, and convenience store salesmen had pretty faces with delicate features.

Driving back to Santa Fe through a glorious early autumn, down the long grassy prairie stretches and around the canyons and cliffs going into Taos, we were silent. As I drove, Mike kept his hand on my leg, and from time to time he leaned over and nestled his head on my shoulder.

The silence was wonderful, full of open-hearted love that expressed itself without words. Looking out at the natural splendors, the endless clumps of deep green juniper and piñon extending back to the crenellated sides of far-off mesas, ocher-toned in this magic light, overhead a procession of white cloud islands moving slowly toward the horizon, I asked myself how this happened? How did this healing of my restless, lonely soul take place?

Chapter Ten

Tuesday, December 25

A cheerless Christmas for me. In the morning, we open presents, but my heart is not in it. The parents have given Mike clothes—a shirt and a sweater—and me a $100 gift certificate from their favorite bookstore. We give them a framed watercolor of the San Miguel skyline, painted by a friend of ours. I give Mike a pocket-watch with a compass, which he has been wanting, and a set of little boxes that fit into another; the last box has a picture of me in it. He gives me a six-month membership to the gym down the street from our house in Mexico.

Mike makes the best of Christmas morning for his parents' sake, joking and filling our coffee cups and eggnog glasses all around. He and I have decided to go tomorrow to an emergency clinic and try to see a doctor. Weighing heavily upon me now is not only the pain of the frequent and difficult urination, but the prospect that I will be examined and found to be really ill. I hate the routine—the waiting, and then the checking of blood pressure, the weighing in, the peeing in a cup for a sample, the taking of blood. Prostate cancer, Marc had said, and I am starting to believe it.

In the afternoon, we go to the home of Mike's aunt and uncle for dinner. Lois and Jerry live nearby in a similar, but newer, home in a similar, but newer, gated community. Lois is two years older than her sister Sharron, a jovial woman with a large laugh; she loves horses and owns one. Jerry is a retired corporate executive, a dry wit with a permanent long-suffering expression tempered by a wry smile.

Some years ago Lois, apparently weary of homemaking, suddenly announced that she would never wash another dish and since then she serves all her meals, even to guests, even on special occasions, on paper plates. I am curious to know whether this peculiar rule will hold for today, Christmas.

We sit, all of us, including a small assortment of visiting cousins I do not know, at two tables weighed down with lovingly-prepared food, featuring the traditional turkey with the equally traditional accompaniments. We eat, without explanation or excuse, on paper plates with a Christmas tree design. They are the elephants in the dining room, so to speak. The only other time I ate Christmas dinner on a paper plate was in Santa Fe years earlier when I volunteered at a Salvation Army holiday meal for the homeless. We served the dinner on doubled-up flimsy white paper plates, the kind with a fluted edge in a sort of swirl pattern. Afterwards, eating the leftovers with the other volunteers, I felt homeless myself, undeserving of real plates. Now that feeling returns, and with it the sense that this may be the first of many future Christmases in which I join the ranks of the poor, the sick, the destitute, and the old at paper plate dinners.

Later, I ask Mike if he has noticed anything different about me. "I haven't had to run to the bathroom all afternoon."

His eyebrows go up. "Sounds like the Mexican antibiotic may be working," he says. What I don't tell him is that I am training myself to hold the pee in and trying to ignore the urgency to go.

I still feel awful. I forgo a glass of wine, but sip on a scotch-and-water to take my mind off the dull ache in my penis.

Wednesday, December 26

*O*n the morning after Christmas, we take Marc's advice and go to a health center. In the crowded waiting room, Mike opens a magazine and puts it between us to cover half of his lap and half of mine, and we hold hands under it.

This treatment facility is in a suburban shopping mall. On this day after the holiday, it is as if a great throng of working-class people have waited to get sick until the obligatory festivities of the season have been put away. The young man across from us in a clean garage mechanic's jumpsuit pats the arm of the woman next to him, a plump woman around his age who seems stuffed into a pair of too small black slacks. A thin African American woman with flecks of gray in her bushy hair chews gum and stares vacantly out the window at a shoe store across the way. Behind us, a weary middle-aged mother repeatedly reins in her restless twin boys, who look to be around ten and clinically hyperactive. A teenage boy wearing headphones that are connected to some mysterious place on him where, apparently, music originates, holds a wad of Kleenex to his bleeding nose.

On these uncomfortably hard turquoise leatherette seats, we wait and wait. Finally, my name is called, and Mike and I enter another holding area. A nurse takes my blood pressure, weighs me, and sends me into the restroom for a urine specimen. Then we wait again.

At last, we are shown into an examining room to wait for the doctor. The bare walls shine with white enamel, slightly blue or green in the light, lit from above by ice blue-tinted fluorescent tubes that send light glinting off two clunky chrome chairs and a stainless steel table covered with thin white paper. This is a frosty world: there might as well be a thin layer of snow on the cheap gray speckled floor tiles.

The doctor is a short woman in her early fifties, brisk, brusque, efficient. She rules these examining rooms, which reflect her manner: cool and spare. Her every word seems measured, as if each is coming from a medicine bottle dropper. When I tell her my symptoms, frequent and painful urination, she barely looks me in the eye. It is only noon, but she appears to be tired and put upon, as if she has been up all night and is waiting for a replacement that should have been here an hour ago.

A bacterium has been found in my urine, which would explain the urinary tract infection. But she is concerned that there might be a larger issue. When I show her the box of antibiotics I bought in Mexico and tell her I have not been feeling much better on them, she cuts me off in mid-sentence.

"That's because these are not antibiotics—they are some kind of antiseptic for the bladder," she says, on the edge of impatience.

She hands the box of pills back to me in a way that suggests the examination is nearing an end and she is beginning to clean up the room.

"Can you examine my prostate to see if it is enlarged?"

"No," she says at once, as if she has been waiting for the question. She explains that if there is an infection, which there apparently is, a digital examination would spread it. I try to connect with her when our eyes meet briefly, but she remains emotionless, her face neither smiling nor frowning.

"Look," she says, finally, "this could be quite serious. You have to promise me that you'll see a urologist as soon as possible." She gets out a notebook to make a referral. When I tell her that we are returning to Mexico in three days, she shrugs and repeats that I need to see a urologist. Meanwhile, she writes me a prescription for Ciprofloxacin, an antibiotic—"a real one"—that I will need to take for two weeks.

In the car, which is Sharron's late model Acura on loan to us during our visit, Mike and I look at each other for a long moment. I cannot remember seeing this much love in his eyes before. Somehow I had thought that my becoming ill, a harbinger of senilitude, would cause him to drift away from me. Now I am beginning to see that just the opposite could happen.

The sun is out, but there is a chill in the air. We linger in the huge mall parking lot as shoppers stroll past our car carrying bags and boxes filled with clothes and electronics, delayed or exchanged Christmas presents.

"We'll get through this, don't worry," he says. I reach out for his hand and lower my eyes, feeling a mixture of shame and gratitude. I wish we could go back two weeks. I wish this was not happening.

❦

I knew you long before you came into my life. I have seen your eyes in the eyes of other young men. I encountered you on the train once from Florence to Padova. You were the young man in the next seat, l'angelo di amore, *who said nothing, but fell asleep reading a magazine about cars.*

"Sei in viaggio per Padova?" was all I said to him before he drifted off. "Ma, certo," he said back to me with a half-smile. Of course—all of us on this train are going to Padova. Certo! Certo! Ma, certo, *can I tell you of my longing? Stay awake, and I'll tell you the story of my life. How I almost died three times and was saved by your*

brother angels, my guardians. Stay up with me so I can tell you how I have searched so long and so hard to be a man. What you find so effortless that it is almost banal. Keep watch with me as we speed through this countryside of ruined brown villas so I can feel the companionship I crave. Hold my hand—don't let me be here alone in this great pool of beauty and feel stranded, feel as if I am drowning. Certo! *Yes, certainly—certainly!* Certo! *But what is certain? Hold me. Touch me, lost youth—for you are my own lost youth that I recognized in the sacred folds of your Levis between your young legs. It is my youth, surely—* certo*—that haunts me so that wherever I go, you are there.*

When I sit down, thinking I am at rest at last, I look next to me to see you, with your sandy wild hair and your impossibly long eyelashes. Certo. *I leave, you leave, the train pulls out—I am safe. And there at the entrance of the* tabacchi, *there near the telephones, at the door of the bar, where the smell of caffè comes strong through the wide station: there you are once more, with skin-tight pants and the ass of an athlete showing through. There you are with black brows like winging blackbirds on a pale face—I see you again, I recognize you.*

Your way is to not notice me, or to turn your head just a little so my eyes can drink in the look of your skin, your hair, your body. It is our secret. We know each other, but on this plane of existence we prefer to stay in our separate skins, to nod assent, but to avoid union—no, to avoid contact of any kind. Certo! *It would be too powerful. We would die. Still, I embrace you with all my heart. Your beauty overcomes me—*certo!

Chapter Eleven

Eight Years Before

Mike wanted a dog. We talked it over briefly, with me giving some of the usual objections parents make—"someone is going to have to feed the dog," "the dog will need shots and check-ups and…and training"—but his mind was set.

One day after work Mike pulled up in the driveway and honked for me to come out. "Come with me to the animal shelter," he said.

"Is today the day?"

"Maybe. I was just there and saw one I liked. Something about the eyes—our eyes met, you know, and it was like we recognized each other. Anyway, I want you to see. Let's hope the one I was looking at is still there."

When we got to the shelter Mike insisted I walk up and down the aisles of doomed dogs, some of them old and sick, others young and frisky, but already beat-up by life and outraged at being penned in this place. He wanted to see whether I was attracted to the same dog he had tentatively picked out.

"This one?" I asked him, pointing to a middle-aged mutt with long white hair and hopeful eyes. Mike shook his head no. It occurred to me that this might be a test to see how well I knew my boyfriend. He had spoken a couple of weeks earlier about a Rottweiler, which surprised me because Mike's mild manner did not seem to match such a potentially ferocious breed. But there were no Rottweilers here, in any case.

I got to a pen with a noisy, medium-sized, stocky black dog that looked vaguely wolfish. When I glanced at Mike, who was smiling down at the "blackie," I knew this was the one.

We named her Milly after the turn of the Millennium, which was upon us at the time. She was about a year old when we brought her home. As I write this, ten years later, she is asleep under my desk.

Not long after Milly became part of the family, Mike told me he wanted to take a road trip by himself, with Milly. He would take a few days and drive from Santa Fe south through New Mexico and over into Arizona all the way down to Puerto Peñasco, also known as Rocky Point, just across the Mexican border. I was uneasy with his plan to go off alone on such a long journey—what if he had car trouble or an accident, or what if he suffered a seizure on the highway? I tried to put these thoughts out of my mind and supported his decision. After all, Mike was an adult, I told myself, and it would do no good to our relationship if I hovered over him constantly, trying to keep him out of harm's way.

Still, I was uncomfortable with him leaving. Even as I kissed him good-bye, I noticed that my hand was covering my heart, as if to settle my anxiety. This would be the first time we would be apart for several days since we began living together. As he drove away from the house, Milly's snout catching the breeze out the passenger window, I had that same sinking feeling I had had so many times before: he is leaving me...will I ever see him again?

He returned a week later, Milly in tow and fully bonded to him, but my apprehensions had been well-founded, it turned out. Lying together on our bed propped up on our elbows, he told me what had happened. On the trip down, heading west out of Gallup, he encountered heavy road construction and the highway narrowed down in progressive stages until there was only one lane of traffic. There, feeling like he was in a quickly closing vice, he experienced his first panic attack. Dizziness came over him, his heart raced, his hands turned clammy, and his skin went tingly. He thought he was about to have a seizure in the middle of the traffic and noise and construction, unable to pull over and stop, and that added to his panic.

Once out on the open road again, the panic subsided and he was back to normal. But it struck again on a skyway overpass on one of the Phoenix freeways—the feeling that he was about to have a seizure and would be not able to pull out of the fast-moving single-file traffic.

As he told me this my own heart raced. I leaned over and held him tightly to me, almost as much to comfort myself as to comfort him.

He and Milly had enjoyed camping out on the warm sandy park grounds at Puerto Peñasco on the Sea of Cortez. Milly had played fetch-the-Frisbee with him and had chased ducks into the water, which she seemed to find endlessly interesting. But on his way back to Santa Fe, on another of the freeways around Phoenix, Mike had another attack and had to pull over to the side of the road. By the time he got home he had begun to be concerned.

"Do you want to do something about this?" I asked. "Do you want to see someone or talk to someone?"

"I don't know. Let me think about it."

Later he told me he knew he was basically in excellent health, so those panic episodes were like emotional waves on otherwise tranquil waters. If that feeling came again, he would work through it by calming himself down and reminding himself that it would soon pass.

These panic episodes, never so fully felt that he would pass out or injure himself, continued with diminishing frequency and intensity for the next two or three years, until they stopped completely. But they set up a pattern of worry in me that I carried around for a long time.

༄

Thursday, December 27

I am doing much better because of the Cipro, but my symptoms, frequent and difficult urination, persist.

Sharron gives me some little red pills called Uristat that turn my pee orange (again). These are pills to ease urinary tract infections. With women, these infections are fairly common, she says, suggesting that in men they are not. I learn later that with men, such a problem is usually an indication of something much more serious. But I am grateful for the red pills, which seem to help my pee come out better and faster.

Mike and I get on two of the house phones and call Marc in Dallas. He says he is glad I saw a doctor and reminds me that the antibiotic may take care of the illness, but there is still the cause, and I will have to have that looked at the minute I return to Mexico.

I see only the back of your head from here, stopping to gaze at you at your desk on this chilly morning, checking your mail. The times when I stumble upon you and you do not see me are the best moments. Now I make a step over to one side and see half of your beautiful face, so concentrated on what you are composing at the computer. May the angels keep you just like this, just the way you look this morning as a shaft of sunlight slices into the room. You turn and see me looking at you and you smile at me. In that split-second you have caught me gathering your beauty to my hungry eyes; you have caught me loving you.

Eight Years Before

Autumn came again to Santa Fe. The Sangre de Cristos shimmered gold with aspens in the soft, strong afternoon light. I had committed for a book tour to promote *The Way of the Traveler*, and set out for New York. Without Mike at my side, it was more like work than the self-congratulatory adventure it might have been. I had so wanted him to hear me speak and see me sign books in bookstores at Rockefeller Center and in Greenwich Village, and later in Washington, D.C.

While I was touring, he drove with Milly up to Minneapolis to visit his parents. We met there after my appearances in Chicago, the last stop on the tour and we drove together back to Santa Fe on the endless flat highways through Iowa and Nebraska and eastern Colorado.

Through the year that followed, my feelings for Mike deepened. He seemed to be feeling the same way toward me. We were practically inseparable when we were not working—me on magazine articles and an anthology assignment, he at the hotel, where he had been promoted to bar-tender, a lucrative job in urbane, cash-flush Santa Fe.

We took yoga classes together at the Community College, trekking out south of town to the campus several times a week. In the evenings, we went out with a widening circle of friends or by ourselves to movies. Mike would save some popcorn in the bag and hide it under his jacket, then in the parking lot he would come behind me and shower me with popcorn. I always knew the popcorn was coming, but always was surprised to have it hit my hair and cascade down my shoulders. The popcorn spray was so funny to me that I invariably broke up in paroxysms of laughter.

A kind of comfortable mood settled around us. For all I knew, Mike could meet some guy at the bar, fall in love, and take off as easily as he had come into my life. But more and more that seemed to be only a remote possibility.

He came home to me every night, sometimes in the early hours of the morning. Whether I was awake or asleep, he would spread his night's earnings out on a corner of the bed and count the bills. One little pile for twenties, another for tens, another for fives, for ones. He was immensely proud of himself for supporting himself and having enough left over to put away. I began to admire not only his willingness to work, but also his practical wisdom about money—managing it, spending it with care, and saving it. I had never been good with money, probably because my parents, children of the Great Depression bequeathed their sense of deprivation to me; growing up, there never seemed to be enough money. For eight years I had lived as a monk under the vow of poverty, when I did not use money at all. In financial matters, I had always been an innocent.

One evening we went to a bookstore to hear an author named Ken Luboff speak about his book, *Live Well in Mexico: How to Relocate, Retire, and Increase Your Standard of Living*. For us, this was a social commitment as well as an opportunity to be informed, since Ken was the former owner of the publishing company that had commissioned me to write *The*

Way of the Traveler. We could not have known that Ken's talk that evening would change our lives.

At a coffee shop after the presentation, we sat quietly sipping café lattes and sharing a big gingerbread cookie.

"What are you thinking about," I asked Mike, finally.

"Mexico," he said. "How about you?"

"Mexico. Do you think we really could do it?"

His face had a faraway look, almost as if he was trying to imagine a life so completely different from what he had ever experienced.

Beginning in November of that year, as the presidential election ended—but the occupant of the presidency was in still question—our lives suddenly accelerated. I had been in contact for several months with Beverly Nelson, a psychologist in Dallas who had gotten in touch with me at the suggestion of her tour operator. Beverly had been taking people on personal growth retreat-journeys to places around the world—Bali, Machu-Pichu, the Galapagos Islands—and her tour operator, who had read an advance copy of *The Way of the Traveler*, thought we might work together in some way. Now we were seriously discussing, on the phone and through email letters, setting up a retreat center somewhere.

Mike and I decided to take a trip to Mexico as a vacation but also to scout out possible places to live and set up the retreat business we had dreamed about since we began seeing one another. We had heard a great deal about a place called Todos Santos, near the southern tip of Baja California, supposedly a tropical paradise and a haven for artists, hippies, surfers, and spiritual types.

We drove to Los Angeles, where we saw friends, then flew to La Paz, the capital of Baja California Sur, rented a Baja Bug, an old Volkswagen Beetle with the top cut off and the engine souped-up to navigate deserts and beaches, and drove across the breadth of the state to Todos Santos, only an hour away.

Todos Santos, we quickly learned, was a lovely place but without much in the way of an infrastructure that would support the kind of business we were contemplating. We wanted to offer guided retreats to people from the United States, especially, and other countries, and that would necessitate a certain amount of international communication. The waiting time for a phone line in Todos Santos, we were told, was four years. At the town's one Internet café, I spent the better part of a morning waiting for pages to come up; when they did, it was as if they emerging from a pool of cyber molasses. Since then, of course, with the rapidly developing technologies of cell phones and the Internet, that little jewel of a town has become more attractive to people who want to not only retire or surf, but to work.

After three days, most of the time spent walking the same three or four streets and seeing the same sights, we flew to the mainland of Mexico, to Guadalajara, then bussed to two Spanish Colonial mountain towns I remembered visiting thirty years earlier—Guanajuato and San Miguel de Allende. San Miguel was the subject of Ken Luboff's book, the one that had sparked our curiosity in Santa Fe. We spent one day and night in Guanajuato, the world-famous seventeenth century mining town and one of the wonders of Mexico, then hurried on to San Miguel.

Saturday, December 29

This morning, I have used up all the little red Uristat pills that Sharron gave me to ease the pain of peeing. When I ask her for a few more, she gives them to me, but says, suspiciously, that I should be feeling a lot better by now. Is she worrying that her son is headed down a spiraling path with me that will end in his being stuck, at his young age, with an invalid partner? The on-and-off fever has left me, but Sharron is right: I should be feeling better than I do.

Mike and I talk about plans for when we return to Mexico. Should we call Claudia, the doctor who knows us and whose office is up the street from us? Should we get an opinion from our Colombian friend Cesar, who is both an acupuncturist and a medical doctor? How will we find a urologist, and how long will we have to wait to see one?

In the afternoon, we pack our suitcases and end up stretching out on the bed. I fall asleep in Mike's arms. How could I ever go through this without him? I feel safe here, next to his heart, feeling him breathe. Asleep, his hand goes to the warm nest between my legs and it is as if he is healing me down there.

Chapter Twelve

How would it be, then, if my sex was damaged beyond repair and I could not express my love for you with the instrument of my love? Must we from now on settle for petting and kissing and holding each other close against the storms of life ignoring, somehow, this lifeless thing hanging here? How would it be for me never again to feel the thrill of stiffness at the root of myself?

Once many years ago in Florence I strolled through the Piazza della Signoria, where the outdoor copy of the David guards the area in front of the Palazzo Vecchio. There he was in all his magnificent marble youngmanhood—and there we were, throngs of tourists with cameras looking up at a giant fifteen-year-old boy, nude and resplendent. A hundred, two-hundred flushed tourist faces. But here is the strange part: as I walked through the Signoria toward the Piazza Santa Croce, my favorite outdoor space in Florence, I observed something about the small plaster David copies being sold by the souvenir vendors. As I progressed down the alleys, I noticed that the penises on the David got bigger, as if the great statue was having a sexual swelling. Was it only my imagination, or were the penises actually larger and more exaggerated as I went along? It was as if the collective thoughts of all the tourists focused on that beautiful member were adding inches and girth to it.

My penis has been my gift to you—and now?

༺༻

Eight Years Before

Something changed in us as we walked through this magical place, San Miguel, which looked to me like a smaller, more colorful version of Rome. We seemed to be smiling all the time, amused and delighted at the town's ambience, which was soft, slow, and aglow with warm light. Even at this time, in late November, the sun shone all day long in a cloudless deep blue sky.

"This is like Santa Fe, but without winter," Mike joked.

It was like Santa Fe in many other ways, as well. Art was everywhere, in tiny mom-and-pop galleries, in artist studios and antique shops around the town's center, and in the streets and parks, where painters sat surrounded by their canvases set up on low stone *bancos* or around fountains.

As in Santa Fe, the heart of town was a plaza, called the *Jardin* (Garden), the locus for all public activity and, to see the number of young lovers holding hands and kissing on the park benches in the shade of deep green laurel trees, private activity, as well. All of the area in the Centro was remarkably familiar to us from living in Santa Fe—one street that edged the *Jardin* was Calle San Francisco, the same as Santa Fe's San Francisco Street bordering its Plaza.

"I could get used to this," I said over a bowl of *Sopa Azteca* at a small family-run restaurant two blocks off the *Jardin*.

"I like it," Mike said. He scooped up some *salsa pico de gallo* with a hot corn tortilla. "Let's look for a place to rent."

"What?"

Mike shrugged and heaped more of the spicy sauce on his enchiladas. I just stared at him. Our mood was such that everything seemed possible, even renting an apartment in one of these grand old colonial buildings, with their high ceilings and arches and colonnaded courtyards draped with cascades of peach-colored bougainvillea.

Mike bought a copy of the English newspaper, circled a rental that looked interesting, and called the owner from a pay phone on the *Jardin*. We spent the rest of the afternoon combing through streets looking for the place that was advertised. We never found the apartment, but we got to see neighborhoods off the beaten track and began to feel excited about the idea of living in San Miguel.

On the morning of our last day, we emailed Beverly from an Internet café and told her where we were and what we were experiencing. She sent back a reply at once saying that she had been to San Miguel the year before and loved it. She was pleased about the prospect of moving here together to start a retreat center.

When it was time to leave San Miguel, we checked out of our hotel and took a cab to the bus station. It was crucial for us to leave on this particular bus to Guadalajara, because everything was timed to the minute for connecting by air to La Paz in the Baja, and from there to Los Angeles. If we missed any one of the connections, we would need to change reservations and rebook flights. We sat in the bus station and reviewed what we had seen and done over the previous two days. The bus would leave at 3:40 pm.

"What time is now?" Mike asked me.

"We have plenty of time—it's 3:15."

We continued to talk, beginning to vision out a plan for moving, going over our finances, discussing our commitments back in Santa Fe, wondering about leaving our friends. Mike asked me again for the time.

"3:15," I said. We stared at one another for a split second, alarm and fear draining us white. "Oh, my God, my watch stopped."

Mike dashed away. Half a minute later, he was back.

"The bus just pulled out. I'll try to catch it." He disappeared again.

I got the bags together and rushed to the station departure ramp through a gaggle of passengers who had just disembarked from another bus. Mike ran up to me breathless.

"They're waiting for us—let's go!"

Chapter Twelve

The bus had pulled out of the station and was rolling out toward the main road. Mike ran after it, yelling for it to stop, and when it did not, he ran in front of it as the bus was about to enter traffic. The bus driver slammed on the brakes. We got on board to the obvious amusement of some of the Mexican passengers, who must have been mentally composing for their friends the story of two crazy gringos running after a bus.

Later, Mike and I joked that my watch stopping—it had never ever stopped before that afternoon—might have been a sign that San Miguel did not want us to leave. But we knew there was a serious side to the joke, and found that we had became still and uncommonly quiet for the remainder of our trip.

We returned to Los Angeles the day before Thanksgiving. The next afternoon we went to the home of my old friends Pancho Kohner and his wife Maggie for Thanksgiving dinner. Pancho is a film producer and director who made a string of popular movies in the 1970s and 1980s, many of them starring Charles Bronson. I had met him twenty-five years earlier when his father, the pioneering talent agent Paul Kohner, brought us together—he to produce and me to write a screenplay based on the curious story of Maximilian and Carlota, briefly the Emperor and Empress of Mexico in the 1860s. Maggie is a hard-working M.D. with a specialty in dermatology, the embodiment of Irish colleen loveliness.

Pancho's famous mother, Lupita, was also at dinner that day. I have known her as long as I have known Pancho. She is a diminutive, handsome woman, a former movie actress who was the star of the first sound film made in Mexico, *Santa* (1934). Doña Lupita—the celebrated Lupita Tovar, whose face once appeared on a Mexican postal stamp—was in her nineties, the survivor of a glorious Hollywood past that included friendships with virtually every film personality of the studio period in the United States and the Golden Age of Moviemaking in Mexico. I had tremendous respect for her. This was the first time she had met Mike.

Lupita looked at me oddly all through dinner, I thought. I tried not to take her unusual demeanor personally, but after the meal, as I was helping Maggie with the dishes, I mentioned it to her. Maggie explained that Lupita had not known about my sexual preference, and, seeing Mike and getting the lay of the land, was trying to deal with her surprise.

"And disappointment?" I asked Maggie.

"Oh no, not a bit. Remember what she's seen and experienced, being in show business all her life," Maggie said with a wink. "It's just that she didn't know."

Later, when I was alone with Lupita on the couch, she patted my hand and said, "Joseph, I like your friend—he is a very nice young man." It was her way of acknowledging the sexual identity I had always kept hidden from her, and giving me her approval.

The whole episode with Lupita that day unbalanced me. It started me off on a kind of examination of conscience, asking myself whether I had been dishonest with the people in my life, toying with them, presenting myself as someone I was not. Certainly, my closest friends knew I was the way I was, and knew that to keep a job at a college in a small town at that time I had to disguise my sexuality or try to "pass" as a heterosexual. I had been as enigmatic as possible with those outside my immediate circle to protect my reputation.

I had women friends and went out with them to social functions, especially the public gatherings connected with the college. But I could not declare my true self—I just could not.

Now, driving back to Santa Fe with Mike at my side, I realized in a kind of crisis moment that his presence in my life represented the ultimate blowing of my cover, my statement to the world that I am a homosexual and a lover of young men. For me, a child of a small town in the 1950s, with its narrow-minded attitudes, this was a big step. If I was to have this love, I would be redefining myself in a fundamental way. Mike was the point of no return for me.

Something shifted in me on that trip. When we returned to Santa Fe I found myself determined to come out of hiding and declare myself sexually. As if a light had switched on, I realized that I owed it to my friends to pull myself out of the shadows of the sexual-preference limbo to which I had assigned myself out of fear. My parents were gone, but I would need to reveal myself to my brother and his wife and the many cousins spread across my Italian-American familial landscape. I owed it to Mike, as well, for him to be seen not as my young buddy, but as my lover.

Around that time, perhaps propelled by the dawning of this new willingness to identify myself as a homosexual, everything seemed to speed up. I flew to Texas to meet Beverly for the first time and over two days we sketched out a program for a retreat center in Mexico. A few weeks later, Mike and Beverly flew to San Miguel, found a perfect place to live and conduct retreats. By the middle of February, Mike and I had sold or given away most of our belongings, packed our two cars with what was left, and, with the cats Madre and Ki and Milly, we headed south to the middle of Mexico.

Everything moved so quickly around that time that we had no real opportunity to feel what we were doing. I was leaving a whole life behind, not only a geographical place—I had lived in Santa Fe through my entire adult years—but also an identity. Mike was leaving the state where he was born and raised, and where he had studied and begun his career as a healer. Maybe it was best that we did not have a chance to reflect much on the enormity of the change we were embarked upon; we might have been frightened into immobility, like scared rabbits.

Not the least of what we were turning our backs on was the warm relationship we enjoyed with our dear Diane, who had become closer to us than the sister neither of us ever had. For both Mike and me, saying good-bye to Diane was the most difficult part of our leaving Santa Fe.

But the prospect of a new life in a new country overtook the pain of parting. Driving down to the border through the back roads of New Mexico and into Texas, we could hardly contain our excitement. Were we really doing this? What if things did not work out? Could we ever go back? We were riding on a ribbon of asphalt, but it seemed to both of us like a razor's edge.

A few miles after we crossed the border at Eagle Pass into Piedras Negras, the chill of February lifted and the strong Mexican sun warmed the air. We rolled the windows down and felt the thrilling new breeze of adventure on our faces.

༄

Sunday, December 30

We fly back to Mexico on an early flight through Houston. The trip is much less stressful than the trip up to the States, no doubt because Christmas is over and the travel madness is over. In the Mexico City airport, we buy our bus tickets to Queretaro, then, having to wait almost an hour for the next departure, find a restaurant and eat a late breakfast. I have to leave the table twice during the meal to pee. I am feeling tired and a little confused, which I try to hide from Mike by chatting and joking. On the bus, Mike is wide awake and deeply into one of his school books. I begin reading a three-week-old issue of the New Yorker I have brought with me, but fall asleep three paragraphs into a story.

When we reach Queretaro, we decide to save time and hire a cab for the fifty-kilometer ride back to San Miguel. I am feeling steadily better with each kilometer, but not entirely well. In the taxi, Mike and I decide to find a urologist as soon as the New Year's holiday is over.

Monday, December 31

I had wanted to spend this day in quiet reflection, but I find myself working at the computer and puttering around the house. Maybe, unconsciously, I am avoiding reflection, since I already know what fears might emerge in me in the absence of distraction. At night, we have a few friends over and I lead the group in a ritual that we have been talking about doing since Thanksgiving. Each of us will write a list of the year's bad things, then we will burn the slips of paper outside on the patio in a large wok.

I write without hesitation on one slip of paper, "death, disease, lack, limitation, illness, suffering"—and realize as I stare at the list that these are the "human illusions" that the American mystic Joel Goldsmith, whose philosophy was formed by Christian Science, said are not part of the spiritual experience. According to Joel, we are spiritual beings for whom anything less than perfection is simply the "malpractice" of the human condition, mirages that have no basis in reality. I have been listening to Joel's "Infinite Way" lecture tapes for over thirty years. Now, suddenly, the words leave some area of my head and go onto the paper without my thinking about them.

After the ritual burning, we write down on new slips of paper what we would like to have in the New

Year. I write, "good health, prosperity, more love for Mike," and can think of nothing else. We fold these and put them in a pocket nearest our hearts. I feel terribly sad. The night is clear and crisp, jacket weather. We walk from the house to the *Jardin*, about six blocks away, with two bagged bottles of wine, which we share among us like college students. But I cannot seem to get into the spirit of things. We watch a dazzling display of pyrotechnics—to bring in the New Year, the town elders have commissioned not one but two *castillos de torres*, literally castle towers, wooden scaffolds three-stories high fitted with spinning wheels of sequentially exploding fireworks. We dodge the random gushers of sparks spilling above and around us. The fireworks' sputtering whooshes of greens and reds and whites are the colors of the Christmas season and also, in layered symbolism, of the Mexican flag. For an hour among a throng of cheering people, with the *Jardin* lit up like day, I forget I may be terribly sick.

By 1:30 in the morning, Mike and I are in bed. Lying there, listening to him breathe, I wonder whether my wishes for the New Year will be granted.

Antinous, I have read, may have drowned himself in the Nile when he was twenty to preserve forever the memory of himself as a young man in the mind and heart of the Emperor Hadrian. Such was his love for the older man that he would sacrifice his life to be an eternally youthful lover. Such was Hadrian's' love for the younger man that, inconsolable at his loss, he made him a god.

Chapter Thirteen

Wednesday, January 2, 2008

Suddenly, we are back in the workaday world. With the interruption of the holidays behind us, Mike makes an appointment for me with a urologist at San Miguel's Hospital De La Fe for tomorrow. I am pleased he is taking a more active role in my health crisis. I am thinking that he wants to make the appointment because he sees that I am in a vaguely distracted state.

We seem to be acting automatically out of some deep sense of panic. Fear possesses us. I gaze into Mike's green eyes and think I see mirrored back the rags and bones of my own mortality. I look at him and imagine how he will be without me.

We are lying in bed, the cold January air filling the room, wanting for sleep to come.

"What are you thinking about?" I ask him.

"Nothing," he says. Then, as if he is pouring out a confession, "I didn't think this would come so soon, all of this...all of this. I wanted it to come later, much later." He looks at me, fixes on my eyes in the near darkness, stretches his arm lovingly across my chest and holds me like that.

Never to grow old. You said something yesterday—that in the photograph from three years ago I sent you last week, you looked so much younger. Are you feeling it, as well, this unkind march of time through our lives?

I look into your loving eyes as we lay next to each other on the bed, shoeless but otherwise fully clothed, on this Saturday afternoon with buttery slabs of sunlight falling over us. My gaze goes to your brown hair with its golden streaks and I wonder when I will be able to detect a silver strand there, then more. Already, now, you are a man and not the boy whose face left me breathless and agitated. Now you bring me a deeper pleasure, seeing you like this, your placid features grown more mature, even softer now in this warm, pale yellow light.

My hand goes to yours the way it did on that night so long ago, that first night when love was only a seed of possibility, a glint of a divine promise, the merest chance, a desperate hope. Your fingers twine in mine. My eyes close. I listen to you breathing lightly, still impossible to believe you are here with me.

On her bed at the foot of our bed Milly lets out a long sigh as she makes herself more comfortable. Together, we float into the misty lands of slumber.

◦∽

Chapter Thirteen

Thursday, January 3

We arrive at Hospital De La Fe, a small private hospital financed by a group of doctors from San Miguel, Queretaro, and nearby Celaya, an industrial city about a forty-minute drive from San Miguel. Over the past twenty years, because of several small medical schools and clinics that have sprung up there, Celaya has gotten a reputation for offering good health care. Several Celaya doctors travel to Hospital De La Fe in San Miguel two or three times a week to meet patients. The doctor we are to see today is from Celaya.

The hospital hallway is dimly lighted from glass brick skylights in the ceiling, which is the floor above. Two young Mexican women are sitting behind a metal desk, chatting and snacking from a tiny bag of corn chips. They are practically in the dark. We tell them we have an appointment with the urologist. One of the young women, about twenty with her black hair in a bun, looks at me blankly for a moment, then explains that the doctor comes to San Miguel only on Mondays, Wednesdays, and Fridays. Our appointment is for the next day. It is some indication of the fuzzy thinking brought on by our fears that we have gotten the days mixed up.

I feel a kind of reprieve, but also a sense of impatience rising in me. Meanwhile, my symptoms are still very much with me. Before leaving the hospital, I need to go to the restroom to pee.

I am putting away your tee-shirts, washed and folded by Belen, our housekeeper, and trying to understand why I am troubled and angry. Was it the boy at the restaurant last night, our mesero, *our waiter, the young man of maybe twenty, with his beautiful black hair and his fair face, his slender waist and hips, his full lips. I wanted to stretch my hand out and touch him, which is to say that I wanted to reach and touch the young man within me, the young man that he is, and that you are for me. Now I know: getting older is making me angry. I am enraged at this cruel curtailment of our time together.*

༄

Seven Years Before

Our first year in Mexico required both of us to be resilient and flexible—and good-humored. I had been traveling in Mexico for thirty years, but living in the country was an entirely different experience. Beverly and I spent our mornings working on the LifePath retreat program and the various personal growth activities we would offer; Mike was in charge of the household, overseeing the staff, running errands, making connections with local service providers.

We ate an early *comida*, the Mexican mid-day main meal, around one in the afternoon, then set out to explore our adopted town. In the evenings, we went out to neighborhood restaurants, occasional play-readings, live music performances, or parties given by other gringos. From time to time we were invited to fiestas at the homes of Mexican friends. At these celebrations we began to absorb the real flavor of Mexican culture, with its blazing colors, infectious music, polite customs, and warm ways.

A few months into our new life in San Miguel Mike and I began to drift into an afternoon pattern. After *comida*, we retired to our apartment in the small retreat center complex and rested. Sometimes we made love or simply lay side-by-side, then fell asleep. I noticed that Mike slept on for an hour or more after I got up.

When I mentioned this to him after a week, he said he just felt exhausted in the afternoon. We decided it must be the bottle of beer he was having with *comida* that was draining his energy and making him drowsy. But after a few days of not drinking, the afternoon fatigue still hit him, and it lasted into the evening until we went to bed at night. Not only was he tired, but his usually fair face seemed darker to me. Even counting the abundant Mexican sunshine that filled our days, he was browner than I thought he should be. I began to worry.

And something else: Mike's mood was also darker. He was having trouble finding his place in this new domestic situation. Beverly and I spent our mornings together writing program materials for the LifePath guided retreats we would offer, sorting through and assembling our separate work over the years to come up with a step-by-step model and a script—our new company's "product." As much as I tried to include Mike in this exciting and time-consuming process, it was clear to all of us that at twenty-seven he had not accumulated as much life and professional experience as Beverly and I had. His contributions would have to be of a different kind and at a different time. It occurred to me that Mike might have begun to think of himself as an outsider, and that could be damaging his self-esteem, making him feel rather inadequate. A cloud of unhappiness hung over him, I noticed, and that seemed to be deepening into depression.

Whatever else was happening, Mike's physical health was deteriorating, and I was scared. When we talked it over, I asked him if he thought how he was feeling might have something to do with his seizure medication. He did not think so. But something was going on in him, because he appeared to be getting more tired and darker every day. Somehow, naively, neither of us expected that illness would intrude on our Mexican caper. What would I do if Mike were really sick? Would we need to return to Santa Fe?

Up to now I had never stepped foot in a Mexican hospital, but on the advice of our English-speaking neighbors, I got Mike into the car and we drove him out of Centro, which was the only part of San Miguel we knew, to the Hospital de la Fe, on the main road that ringed the town.

The hospital, with its institutional pea-green walls and dim florescent lighting could have been a set for a Vincent Price horror movie. The creepiness of the place added to my alarm. In this light Mike looked even gaunter and darker. The girl at the desk, half hidden in the shadows near the entrance, asked us politely to wait, then dialed a number on the antiquated telephone. As we waited, I kept giving Mike brave, loving smiles and patting his hand, wondering whether my face was betraying my anxiety.

Moments later, the reception girl came to where we sat on an orange vinyl couch and led us upstairs to the doctor's office. Dr. Sanchez was a short, slender man with a serious expression behind large wire-rimmed glasses. He motioned for us to sit across an old school teacher's desk from him on gray metal folding chairs. After we told him about how Mike had been feeling, he came over to us and asked Mike to stand up. He leaned over, stretched Mike's eyelids open a little, and stared into his eyes.

"You have Hepatitis," he said, pronouncing it "Epa-TEE-tees." "This looks like Hepatitis-A. We don't know how one gets this problem. It could be from eating something. Rest. Sleep. Do nothing for one month. No alcohol, only soups to eat. You are young—you will be fine."

I felt my shoulders drop in relief. Mike grinned wearily. There were answers to these questions. Mike was not in great danger. He was not going to be permanently sick and disabled. I was not going to have to be his caretaker for the rest of his life. He was going to "fine."

Driving home, I held on tight to the steering wheel and started sobbing and laughing at the same time. Mike pulled himself over to me and put his arm around me. I felt a tremendous release of tension, and I could sense it in Mike as well. Without having to say a word, we both knew we were going to be fine, we were going to make it in this new and unfamiliar world.

When we got back to the house, swept up by the euphoria of the moment, I announced that we needed to take a vacation.

"Let's go to New York," I said to Mike, who surfaced momentarily from the torpor of his illness to smile and hold me close to him.

I am remembering the last time you had a seizure, the only time I have seen you seizing. I have never been more frightened, or more completely in love with you. The boy whose face was as familiar to me as my own changed in a few seconds to someone I did not recognize. I was overcome with fear, but calm at the heart of it, certain that the essence of you was still there under the contortion, that compression of your features, the flaying, the falling, the stiffening, the twisting into rigidity.

Chapter Fourteen

On the morning of September 11, I had been at the computer and had seen a report that a plane had flown into one of the towers of the World Trade Building in New York. Beverly had gone to Dallas two days before to see clients there. Mike and I dashed downstairs to turn on the television. By the time we got onto CNN, the other tower had been hit. We watched, speechless, at the sight of black clouds billowing up over lower Manhattan. It all felt so personal to us—we had made plans to visit in three weeks the very places we were seeing in the midst of what looked like a terrible destruction.

When Beverly was able to get through on the phone, we told her the border had been closed. There was silence, then we heard her sobbing softly. "I feel so far away from home," she said, when she could speak again. She already had claimed Mexico as her home and, sealed off from it, marooned in the United States, was overcome with homesickness.

Ironically, Mike and I were experiencing a reverse longing for the world we had left behind, our homeland, after all, which appeared to be falling apart, sealing us off on this side of the border from all we had known, from our past.

Ten days later, in the early evening as he and I were finishing a supper of salad and soup, Mike had a seizure. I had left the table with the dishes and taken them to kitchen area of the large open room that was our living and dining room. He had gone over to the couch. I heard a scraping, rustling noise behind me. When I looked over my shoulder, Mike was crumbled up in the corner on the floor next to the couch, hitting the side of his head against the concrete wall.

I dropped the dishes on the counter and rushed over to him. I had never seen him seize, but I knew instantly what was happening. His arms were flailing and twitching, and the sides of his face were squeezed together as if his face was in a vice, his mouth open in a large oval, making him look like the man in Edvard Munch's painting, "The Scream." The skin on his face and hands had gone ghostly pale and was clammy and cold. The panting sound that came out of his mouth was like a string of short, loud animal groans. He did not look like my Mike — before my eyes he was transforming into someone I hardly recognized.

I gathered him up in my arms and held him tight to try to quell the uncontrollable jerks of his body and the sharp back-and-forth movements of his head. I pulled him closer to me and tried to hold his head steady, but the thrashing continued, forced on by strong involuntary muscle contractions.

"It's alright, everything is okay, you're safe," I said softly over and over again like a mantra. "It's alright, everything is okay, you're safe, I'm with you."

Beverly was at our door and, the minute she saw what was happening, hurried over to us. She helped me hold onto him so he would not hurt himself in the throes of the convulsions. She must have seen how surprised and frightened I was, because she repeated calming words to both of us.

"You're going to be okay, there, there," she said to him. And then, turning to me, "Joseph, he's going to be okay." She had seen seizures many times and had helped people through them.

After about five minutes of this, the storm began to subside. Mike's body jerks came less frequently and were not as violent. His head gradually stopped lashing from side to side. Last to calm down and compose itself was his face — the face I so loved, but could barely find in the dank, blood-drained, compressed mask I now pressed to my chest. Slowly, ever so slowly, I felt his body relax and start to melt. The tight tension in his face muscles left in slow stages, as well. He was breathing heavily.

Then, as he was coming to awareness, the questions began, a hundred of them, repeated over and over: "What happened? How long was I out? Oh, damnit, oh shit. Did I hit my head? How long was I...? Did I hurt myself? Is my head okay? What happened? Did I fall? Damnit, shit. Am I okay? How long was I out?"

I answered his questions one by one, repeating my answers even though he kept asking the same questions again. It was as if he could not hear me or could not understand the words I was speaking.

"How long was I out? Did I bang my head? Damnit. Oh, crap. My head aches...did I hurt myself?"

When she saw that he was out of danger, Beverly left us. Mike and I stayed like that for half an hour until he was completely calmed down. I gave him a glass of water. He took only a sip and put the glass down. He looked at me, a haunted look that was also a mixture of fear, shame, relief, defeat—love.

He fell into my arms and I held him until he started to doze off. I made him comfortable on the couch, then went upstairs for a pillow and a blanket. In the few minutes I was gone, Mike was curled up in a fetal position, sound asleep. I covered him up, tucking the blanket around him, turned the lights off, and pulled a chair over to the couch for myself.

Sitting there in the dark, with only a sliver of light from the lamp outside our window falling across the room and illuminating part of Mike's face, blissful now in repose, I took a deep breath and retraced everything that had happened in the past two hours—two hours! Though I was the picture of composure for Mike's sake, I could feel my heart still racing. All I could think of was the famous phrase from the traditional wedding vows, "...in sickness and in health...." This is what it meant: to be at the side of the loved one no matter what befell, good or bad.

In that moment I silently committed myself to him, to take care of him if needed, to love and protect him, and to be with him for all of what remained for me of this lifetime. I pulled a blanket over my shoulders and, sometime toward morning, fell asleep in the chair.

The next day Mike was fine, if a bit drowsy. When, eventually around lunchtime, we talked about what had happened and what might have caused him to have a seizure after three years of not having one, he admitted that he had been tinkering with his medication, cutting back on the three little pills he was told by his neurologist in Las Vegas to take every night before going to bed. That had been dangerous, of course, and now he determined to get back on and stay on the prescribed dosage.

Beverly, who had returned from the States a few days earlier, suggested another possible cause for the seizure, or at least a contributing cause. As a psychologist, she had seen the effects of the September 11 events on her clients—feelings of helplessness, fear, anxiety, even panic. She wondered whether Mike might be experiencing similar stressful fallout. If so, would it be a good idea to continue with plans for our New York trip? Could the over-stimulation of travel—not to mention the chaotic kaleidoscope of Manhattan, especially at this uncertain, maybe dangerous time—trigger another seizure?

We decided to take the trip, and spent ten glorious days seeing the celebrated sights, reconnecting with old friends, touring museums, eating grandly, getting lost in Harlem, walking incessantly. But New York that first week of October in 2001 was a city in shock. As we made our approach into La Guardia in the early evening, passing the great metropolis on the left, we could see the glow from the bright worklights at Ground Zero, klieg lights trained on the spot to allow round-the-clock crews to remove the debris which once had been the famous buildings. To me, it looked as if a powerful light was shining not into, but out from a hole in the earth. Something enormous had been birthed down there, and the light from that opening in the mother planet still radiated, three weeks after the event.

The next day we got closer to the site from the top of the Empire State Building, squinting into the afternoon sun to try to see something more than a thin trail of smoke and a kind of astonishing absence. It was the only time I have ever waited in line for more than two hours to see an empty space.

A few days later, we hiked into Lower Manhattan to within two blocks from where the World Trade Center complex stood. There, seeing the cranes among the ruins, breathing in the acrid scent of burned electrical wires, we felt the full impact of what had happened.

"I feel...so sad," Mike said, hanging his head on my shoulder.

If something had been born there, it had left not only blood but also a mass of tangled, melted metal in its wake. In the long shadows of late afternoon, with my dear old friend Saliann Kriegsman, who had come up from her home in Washington for the day to be with us, we recited Psalm 91, the ancient prayer of protection, which contains the lines, "*You will not fear the terror of the night, nor the arrow that flies by day, nor the pestilence that stalks in darkness, nor the destruction that wastes at noonday.*" We said it as much for ourselves as for the souls who had converged there on that fateful morning to meet an assignment in annihilation.

Reminders of New York as I remembered it before September 11 hit me when I least expected it. We were sitting in a subway car one day, half-mesmerized by the gentle swaying and jostling of the ride. I looked up at a placard—an ad for a local university, with a smiling coed in the foreground and the legendary New York skyline in the background—except that now the skyline behind her, punctuated by those proud towers, is what jumped into relief. For a moment, I seemed to be in a time warp, and I felt an abrupt shift, a dislodging. Every image of the New York skyline before the event—on post cards, on calendars, on the sides of buses, in commercials, in movies and television sitcoms, even cartoons—was like that, a picture of, as a journalist at the time wrote, "an extinct culture."

Was I somehow linking what had happened in New York to the recent upheavals in Mike's health? I knew it was irrational, but I was feeling an odd tie between the fragility of what had been thought to be unshakable towers of steel and what I had assumed was Mike's unwavering good health. As we stood on a subway platform and stared at the image of the Trade Center buildings on a poster advertising banking services, I wondered if the young man beside me, my lover, so much a part of me by now, was as vulnerable to attacks from life's unpredictable threats as those "unassailable" towers. I looked away, wishing the thought would disappear as easily as the picture disappeared from my sight.

On Saturday night, we decided to walk in the hectic wonderland of Times Square. I knew this would be the ultimate test of Mike's ability to withstand the "over-stimulation" that Beverly spoke about before we left. Certainly nothing was as stimulating to the senses as the rush of standing at 42nd Street and Broadway on a Saturday night, in the midst of a crush of people, with moving colored lights everywhere and giant signs flamboyantly, insistently proclaiming countless products and entertainments.

Mike had told me once that strobe lights were extremely disturbing to him because the feeling he got when high-intensity lights flashed on and off was like the euphoric and helpless feeling at the onset of a seizure. But here we were, picking our way through a virtual combat zone of bright flashing lights, and he was as relaxed and delighted as a child. I, on the other hand, would not let my guard down until, hours later, when we returned to our hotel room in Chelsea and lay side by side in bed, stroking each other gently, as if to bring one another back into our bodies and into connection again.

Our New York excursion, which we had intended as a vacation but ended up as a kind of pilgrimage, nonetheless revitalized us. We returned to Mexico recharged and bursting with a hundred ideas for our future together. But a week or so after we got back and resumed the routine of our life in San

Miguel, I noticed that Mike seemed drift into a mild depression. He was tired much of the time. Whereas before he would think nothing of walking down into the center of town and back from our perch halfway up the hill two or three times a day, now he might amble down to the market at the foot of the hill and trudge back only once a day, at most, and offer an unconvincing excuse for not going out at night. I thought his Hepatitis may have come back.

"You seem awfully unhappy," I said to him finally one night when we were out walking Milly through the backstreets in our hillside neighborhood.

At first he said nothing. As we approached the front door of our house, he knelt down to take Milly's leash off, then stood up and looked at me. "I guess I am," he admitted softly.

When we got inside, we went upstairs to our bedroom and lay together on the bed with Milly between us. "What's wrong?" I asked.

"I don't know if I want this—all this...the retreat business, Mexico. It's like I can't find my place. I don't know if this is what I want to do with my life." He combed his fingers through Milly's thick black neck fur.

"Do you want to go back to the States?" I said, not really wanting to hear the answer. Milly hopped off the bed, as if she sensed the tension growing between Mike and me and had begun to feel vague fears of her own. He kept his eyes on the dog, on the bed covers, on anything but me. When he did not reply, I jumped in again.

"I am feeling committed to this—to the business we're starting, to our business partner, to being here in Mexico. There's nothing for me back there anymore. Besides, I can't move again, not now, not so soon. I just don't have the energy for it."

I reached out for his hand. Always, it seemed, when our fingers intertwined as they had on that first night together, our hearts were immediately joined.

"I'm going to stay," I said. "But that doesn't mean you have to stay."

Mike looked at me, finally, and when he did it was with a deeply troubled and deeply questioning expression.

"What are you saying, then?" he asked.

I could hardly get the words out of my mouth. How I did not want to say or even imagine these things. The thought of Mike going away and never coming back sent a chill of fear through me. I began to feel lightheaded. "If you want to go, I think you should go."

"Where would I go?" He was thinking out loud, entertaining the idea as a distinct possibility. He turned his face away again, as if drifting away from me into a land of his own, a place apart from me where he would begin a new life.

"Back to Santa Fe...maybe California. We have friends in both places. You could set up your practice..." Part of me was regretting I had embarked on this path, but there was no way to unsay what I had said. My stomach grumbled, whether from hunger, since we had not cooked dinner for ourselves, or from the emotional "gut-grind" of the moment.

"Yes, I could," he murmured, grasping my hand more firmly. He looked me squarely in the eye, his brows arching up. "You would let me go, then?"

"I only want you to be happy, Mike. If leaving here and leaving me will make you happy, then…" I heard my voice trail off, my words squeezed in by my feelings.

Without saying more, we got ready for bed. We moved around slowly, each of us enclosed in a deeply personal envelope of thought. He took three little pills from his pill-box, cupped them into his mouth, and chased them down with a long swig from the water bottle next to the bed. I clicked off the lamp on the bedside table and felt him snuggle up next to me, as he always did when we were ready for sleep.

"Thank you," he whispered in the darkness. "Let me think about all this."

I caressed his hair and drew him closer to me. On the eve of his possible departure from my life, we seemed, paradoxically, more intimate and solidly together than ever before. As I drifted off to sleep an image floated across my mind's screen—it may have been a dream—my hand, palm up, opening slowly, nothing there.

Chapter Fifteen

Friday, January 4

Back at the hospital, we wait in the upstairs hallway to see Dr. Juan Carlos Fernandez, the urologist. After fifteen minutes, he opens the door of his little office, greets us in Spanish, and we go in. He is a short man in his late forties, with a trim moustache and a balding head. The office still smells of the cigarette he has put out a few minutes before. The room is cool and bare, with a small wood laminate desk like a student's desk, an examination table, and a tiny bathroom with no door.

Dr. Fernandez has what appears to be a new laptop computer, of which he seems quite proud. Into this he types information about me, something that in the United States would be taken care of by a receptionist with an intake form. He gathers this data in Spanish—he does not speak English. That done, he looks directly at me for the first time.

When I tell him my symptoms, he says immediately that he thinks it might be an infection of the prostate brought on by the jostling of travel. I look blank-faced at Mike, who seems to be thinking the same as I: the preliminary diagnosis is suspect, too easy and obvious. Is the man a quack?

"*Quiero que usted tenga un análisis de sangre—y un examen de ultrasonido,*" Dr. Fernandez says solemnly—he wants a blood test to get a PSA reading and a rectal ultrasound examination to get a picture of my prostate. The PSA (prostate-specific antigen), I will learn later at my own computer, is a secretion of the prostate, the walnut-sized gland enfolding the duct leading from the bladder to the penis. The prostate manufactures PSA all the time, so a small amount of the protein (a reading of between 3.5 and 4) is normal for my age. Cancer cells produce extra PSA, so a higher reading may indicate the presence of cancer. For the ultrasound picture of the prostate, a small "microphone" camera is inserted in the rectum.

With me leaning over the table, my pants pulled down, the doctor takes a digital examination of my prostate. I do not even think to ask him why he would want to do this when the doctor in the States refused to perform the simple exam. Embarrassed and helpless, I glance across the room at Mike with a hurt, little-boy look.

Dr. Fernandez says the American doctor was right to prescribe Ciprofloxacin. He says it as if the American doctor, an obvious lightweight and underling, had taken a shot in the dark and somehow come up with a correct diagnosis of my condition and a reasonable recommendation for treatment. He extends the prescription for another two weeks and adds Xatral OD, a pill that will relax the duct going from the bladder past the prostate, which he says feels enlarged. Forcing a little smile, he tells us that this is serious, but that we should not worry because the medicines will help.

"*No coma chilies ni alimentos picantes,*" he says as an afterthought, showing us to the door. I am not to eat chili peppers or spicy foods.

Mike slips into the driver's seat of the car, puts the key in, then sits back and goes for my hand. "I hated seeing you like that," he says. "When you were leaning over and looking up at me, I felt so bad—I just wanted to go over and hug you." I squeeze his hand and look away, so he will not see me tear up.

In the afternoon, at home, the Xatral begins to work and I have, for the first time in weeks, the exquisite pleasure of completely emptying my bladder. Looking down at the strong stream of urine leaving me, I feel like laughing and crying at the same time. In the back of my mind, I am wondering whether I will need to take pills for the rest of my life just to enjoy the innocent, natural gratification of peeing.

One night as I was writing this book, Mike and I made a bowl of popcorn and watched a movie, The Curious Case of Benjamin Button. *Neither of us was prepared for the impact it would have on us. In it, a man is born old and becomes progressively younger as the years go by. He meets and befriends a young girl; when she reaches maturity—when they are roughly the same age—they fall in love with each other and decide to live together.*

But then the inevitable happens. Day by day she continues to age, he continues to grow younger. Gradually, sadly, they disconnect and go their separate ways. Some years later he reappears in her life, but by now he is the age of her (and his) teenage daughter.

There is more, but what opened our hearts to each other was the film's meditation on the passage of time in two directions. An arc ascending, an arc descending—like us, except that you are ageing along with me. We have met in the precious, ephemeral space of time at the top of the arc to experience a great love.

What if we could stay as we are now? What if we aged only one day for one week of time, or only one month for one year? What if we could stop time altogether and enjoy our endless days sharing our lives together? What if I could live in reverse for thirty years while you did not age at all, and we could meet at the one age you are now and go forward into the future as the twins of time? If we could wave a magic wand over our relationship, would we not choose to bring all the clocks in the world to a standstill so that no more lines would sketch our brows, no more shadows fall under our eyes, no more gray hairs sprout on our bodies, no more thin folds of skin gather under our chins, no more sliding of our faces slowly, slowly down to the corners of our mouths?

We held each other lying like that on the couch after the movie, melted into one other, as if by holding on tightly to the solid flesh of the other we would be holding back time, one protecting the other from the wild rush of fleeing moments. We lay in that way for more than an hour, wordless, each comforting the other against the storm of emotions let loose by the movie's theme.

Saturday, January 5

I wake up at seven o'clock, dress, get on my scooter in the chill dark just before dawn, and drive downtown, to a place a block and a half from the Jardin, for a blood test. The lab is two little rooms on the ground floor of a hotel that caters to Mexican families. The girl who is to take my blood is the new weekend person. She cannot find a vein in either arm, so she takes blood out of the vein in my right hand. The test results will not be ready until after six on Monday evening. Meanwhile, I have black-and-blue marks on my arms where she put the needle in but could not get blood. At home, Mike rubs arnica salve on the marks.

Six Years Before

Two days after I let you go, you came to me with your decision.

All through the day after we talked about breaking up and each going our own way, we kept some distance between us. Mike ran some errands and then took Milly for a long walk in the *Jardin Botanico*, the nature preserve up the hill from our place. I spent most of the day at the computer working on an article for a magazine that wanted a piece on Mexico as a destination for people interested in personal growth. In the evening, still avoiding more of a talk than the usual pleasantries, we went down to the *mercado* for *tacos al pastor*, roasted meat with a selection of fresh salsas. Then we walked back to the house and went to bed.

The next morning we got up and went downstairs to cook breakfast. I cut up a tomato to toss in with the eggs. Mike slipped two slices of bread into the toaster.

"I want to be with you," Mike said. I dried my hands on a dishcloth and looked at him. He waited a moment, then fell into my arms. "Wherever we end up, I just want to be with you."

I was too choked with emotion to say anything. A tremendous wave of relief washed over me. He was not walking out of my life. For now, at least for now, he was staying at my side.

We spent much of the morning talking about how a different living arrangement might help both of us feel more at home in our new country. A few days later, after discussing it with Beverly, we went looking for an apartment and found one only two blocks up the hill. For the first time since our relationship began, we would be living alone together, just us two.

The apartment was on the second floor of a Mexican family's house, two large airy and sunny spaces set in an "L" shape with the landing at the top of the stairs between them. The place had a vaguely unfinished feeling about it. The room on the left had a kitchen at the far end. We divided the room in half, making a kind of sitting room and office at the front, and a cooking and eating area at the back. The other huge room broke down into another sitting area, with our bedroom behind that. We had plenty of space, but it required a creative approach to make it look like a home. Out of wrap-around windows, the views, all the way to the *Centro*, with the fairy-tale *Parroquia* church on the main square, and stretching as far as the lake on the outskirts of town, were spectacular.

The house was owned by Señor Manuel, a descendant of a prominent San Miguel family. He spoke an unusual brand of English, owing to a checkered past that included, curiously, a stretch of time serving in the United States Navy—curiously, because he was a citizen of Mexico, not the US. Manuel was in his mid-seventies; his petite, model-beautiful wife Socorro was in her mid-thirties. With her long ebony hair, delicate features, and perfect figure, she looked more like a visiting movie star than the matron of the house.

Manuel always appeared, morning, noon, and night, as if he had just gotten out of bed after a night of heavy tequila drinking—even though, as far as we knew, he did not drink at all. His wispy white hair was permanently windswept, even on the calmest of days, and his clothes were rumpled and threadbare. He was clever with words, to the point where he made puns that tangled Spanish and English together. Discussing the rent money one day he mumbled, "A peso is very heavy—*pesado*—but a dollar is a pain—*dolor*...so you see, money is always a problem."

There was no heater in the apartment, but in the flurry of moving we somehow had not paid attention to that important detail. In every apartment or house I had ever rented in the States heat was considered part of the package, like floors, ceilings, windows, and doors. But in Mexico, at least here in the high desert, where the weather was almost always mild, heat was seldom included in a rental. The weekend we moved in—it was mid-January—the weather suddenly and uncharacteristically turned damp and cold. The sky clouded over for three days and a cold rain poured down. The apartment became a refrigerator. During the day we stayed warm by taking an occasional hot shower. At night, we moved our mattress into the kitchen, lit the stove's gas oven, and bundled up together among stacks of still-unpacked boxes.

On the afternoon of the third day of cold and wet weather, we were leaving the apartment to go into Centro, jackets zipped up, wool scarves wrapped around our necks and ears, and encountered Manuel at the foot of the stairs.

"What are you two doing for heat up there?" he asked, without a hint of irony. Mike and I looked at each other with expressions that said, *Should we just punch this guy out and move to another place...or let it go?* We let it go. A few hours later the moment became a hilarious memory.

We learned an important lesson from Manuel about patience. Once we complained to him about the telephone company not coming to the house to hook up a line for us.

"I spoke with them yesterday and they said someone would be here today," I told Manuel.

"What did they say exactly, in Spanish?"

"They said *mañana.*"

"There's your problem," Manuel said, scratching his scraggly two-day-old beard. "You must remember that in Mexico *mañana* does not necessarily mean 'tomorrow,' it just means 'not today'."

One morning Manuel brought a dish of Socorro's fresh cornbread up to us and found me sweeping the kitchen floor. Surprised to see a man wielding a broom in his own home, he said he would find us a housekeeper. Later the same day he reappeared with the next-door neighbor, Belen, a thirtyish-looking woman with dark hair pulled back into a bun from a lovely full-moon face. She had the sturdy build of a Mexican mama—she had three children, all of them under ten—and the air of a professionally trained problem-solver. Later we would discover that she had been a well-regarded receptionist in several offices in Centro before starting her family.

After the usual polite introductions, Manuel said, "Tomorrow she will come to clean and cook for you. She will work for three days. If you like her, you can employ her."

I thanked him and said we would be pleased to see Belen again in the morning. Belen's eyes surveyed the place quickly. She looked back at me, smiled modestly, and left. When Mike got back home from his office, he was delighted about the prospect of getting some help with the household chores.

"Let's hope it works out," he said. Then, as his mind clicked at the same time as mine, he added with a cheerful chuckle, "Let's see what happens when she finds out she will be making one bed and not two."

Eager to please us, Belen threw herself into a thorough cleaning of the apartment. Both Mike and I were out all day with work and errands. When we returned, the place was as spotless and put together as a hotel suite—and there was a pot of chicken soup on the stove.

"It's like *Snow White and the Seven Dwarfs*," I said. "You know, like when the dwarfs come home from working in the mines all day?"

"Heigh-ho," Mike joked back.

When we told Belen on the third day that we liked her work and wanted her to be our housekeeper, she seemed surprised.

"*Sí?*" she asked, setting her mop down momentarily and wiping her brow with a wadded-up tissue.

"*Sí, por supuesto!*" Of course we wanted her, I said, trying to hold back my enthusiasm to stay within the conventions of business etiquette.

"*Bueno,*" she said. She stood there with the mop in her hands waiting for me to say something else. From her expression, which suggested that there was another shoe to drop, I guessed it had to do with the relationship between Mike and me.

"*Solomente una cama en la casa,*" I offered. She nodded, agreeing that there was only one bed in the house. *"Está bien contigo?"*

"*Si, todo está bien,*" she said emphatically, everything was okay. That sealed the deal. She smiled briefly, grateful to have the air cleared, apparently, gave me a respectful nod, and got back to work.

From that day Belen became part of our family—and we became part of hers. Her Catholic upbringing apparently did not stand in the way of her keeping house for two men living together in relationship. Smart, honest to a fault, and philosophical about life's ups, downs, and changes, Belen would teach us much over the years about the simple joys of domestic life.

Chapter Sixteen

Spring came quickly on the heels of the bad weather. The sun reappeared, and with it new sprouts on the blood-red geraniums in the pots outside our windows and the banks of orange bougainvillea hugging the walls across the lane from our house. Soon billows of big lavender blossoms on the jacaranda trees swelled up in back yards all around the neighborhood. The hot shower days and open-oven nights were long past.

Belen kept the house immaculate, washed our clothes and dried them in the sun on the line outside our kitchen, and repaired them when they needed buttons or patches. I bought roses and *nardos* at the *mercado* two or three times a week and she set them out in big vases in the living area and the bedroom. Soups and stews waited for us at the end of the day, and fresh, chewy blue-corn tortillas or still-warm *bolios* baked that afternoon at the *panaderia* down the hill.

Mike and I, recommitted to each other in a place that was all our own, were riding high on a wave of contentment. We seemed to be smiling all the time, the way we did in the first few months after we met. I was working on a new edition of *The Way of the Traveler*. Mike was starting his massage therapy practice in earnest at an office downtown that he and Beverly and I rented to house the retreat business. He even had time in the evenings to work at his jewelry bench, managing to turn out some fine-looking rings and bracelets and brooches.

To launch his bodywork practice, he came up with the idea of running a weekly raffle at the upscale salon of a hairdresser friend of ours. The clients who went in to have their hair done entered the raffle by dropping cards with their names and phone numbers into a fishbowl. The weekly winner received a free massage. In two months, Mike had a database of virtually all the well-heeled women in San Miguel. Word spread quickly that he did excellent work. Before the year was out, Mike had built himself a thriving business of his own.

One afternoon that summer he came home from his downtown office with the news that he had decided to become a college student with the goal of getting a Bachelor of Science degree in Natural Medicine.

"When I have that, I think I'd like to go on and become a Naturopathic Doctor," he told me with mounting enthusiasm. He had found a program that he could complete through correspondence on the Internet. Now that we had good Internet service—dial-up had been replaced in town by high-speed cable access that year—obtaining a degree by studying on-line was more of a possibility. The program was offered by a school of natural health in the United States, a pioneer in distance-learning and highly respected for its courses of study in alternative healing.

"How long is it going to take?"

"Four years," he said, "maybe five. Then two more years for the doctorate." My face must have registered astonishment and concern, because he added quickly, "I really want to do this."

"It's an excellent idea," I said, trying to match his enthusiasm. I'll do everything I can to help you." We kissed on that and seconds later he was on the computer filling out his admissions application.

I observed all these leaps in him, admiring the way he poured energy and enthusiasm into his work and into creating a successful venture apart from the retreat business—apart from me. Mike was maturing. The young man I fell in love with four years earlier was now twenty-nine, fully grown up and taking responsibility for himself. Whenever I looked at him during that wonderful spring and summer, I saw both the boy and the man, and felt a surge of pride as, I suppose, a father might feel for a son. My respect for him grew and my admiration, quite apart from my heart-opening love for him, soared. Before my eyes he was developing into an adult with tremendous presence and poise.

The admiration I felt for Mike as a blossoming adult and the newfound elevated self-esteem that he felt following upon his business success lifted our relationship to a new level. At the downtown LifePath offices, we worked side-by-side—he at his bodywork practice, me at my writing and spiritual counseling—mingling our private with our professional lives in such a way that we both experienced the pleasure of a single task shared between us. We shared some clients, as well, and were able to address their healing needs each in our own way.

All the while, Mike's work was expanding and getting deeper. He was becoming an expert at feeling and working with energy. One of the clients we had in common, a woman in her seventies who had suffered with lower back pain for years, told me, "Mike just ran the palms of his hands above my back and found the problem—without even touching me. Then he manipulated some muscles and made the pain go away."

On the verge of turning thirty, that symbolic passage into young adulthood, Mike was reaching a kind of fullness of his personality. He was nearly always happy, pleased with himself, and demonstrably loving to me.

I was approaching a symbolic life passage of my own. In the fall, I would turn sixty.

༄

Monday, January 7

At the LifePath office, I research frantically on the Internet. I email Mike in the next office with a link about *prostatitis*, which, from the symptoms listed, is now what I think I have.

Prostatitis is inflammation or infection of the prostate gland—an organ about the size and shape of a walnut, located just below the bladder in males. The prostate gland produces semen, the fluid that helps nourish and transport sperm. Prostatitis can cause a variety of symptoms, including a frequent and urgent need to urinate and pain or burning when urinating—often accompanied by pelvic, groin or low back pain (MayoClinic.com)

At six in the evening, we go back to Hospital De La Fe for the sonogram. It is as demeaning as Dr. Fernandez's digital examination, given by a chubby, copper-faced male nurse who, judging by his demeanor, does not seem to like Americans. Mike watches sympathetically as the white-coated nurse inserts the probe inside me—at the doctor's recommendation, I have taken an enema an hour before this so no feces will be in the way. A younger man is there, as well. He is cuter and nicer, and seems to want me to have nothing wrong with me. I think of them as kind of Mexican medical counterparts for Mike and me.

The examination lasts about twenty minutes. Afterwards, I dress and Mike and I go to the office down the hall to wait for the results.

"On the way home, let's stop and get some vegetables for tomorrow," Mike says. It is a comment so out of the blue, so disconnected—a way for him to distance himself from the drama at hand, a way to cling to our normal lives?

"Good idea," I say finally, joining him in drifting away from the anxiety of waiting.

The pictures are ready in less than half an hour. The young man, the nurse's assistant, hands them to me in a manila envelope. Is it my imagination, or does he have an apologetic look on his face? I open the envelope immediately and read the results in Spanish: a nodule of six millimeters on the prostate...a biopsy is recommended. A biopsy.

I stare at the four black-and-white pictures, each the size of a credit card. There it is: a little black spot, so small, darker black against the grainy gray of the rest of the prostate. Mike looks at the pictures and sees the spot.

"Well, we really don't know what it is...what it means," he says, as we walk to the car. He slips into the driver's seat of our old Subaru station-wagon.

On the road toward home, I crawl into my head and Mike notices it. I have not shown him the write-up or told him about the word "biopsy." Now, I take a deep breath and say it.

"They are recommending a biopsy."

"Why didn't you tell me that right away?" he asks, on the edge of anger. I feel the car slow down. "You always try to hide things from me. I hate that."

"I didn't want to worry you," I offer feebly. "I'm sorry. Obviously, I'm not thinking straight." For a few minutes we say nothing.

"I'm going to the store to get some vegetables," he says finally. He leaves me off at the house. I decide to go by myself to pick up the results of the blood test. The night is chilly, but I bundle up and drive my scooter over to the clinic.

Two steps outside the lab, I rip open the manila envelope with the results. The normal PSA reading for a my age group is between 3.5 and 4. My PSA reading is 16.5.

Wednesday, January 9

We have an eleven o'clock meeting with Dr. Fernandez, the urologist, at Hospital De La Fe. As before, the faint scent of cigarette smoke lingers in the air. He looks at the blood test results, shakes his head, and tells us what we already know, that the PSA number is dangerously elevated—a sign of possible malignancy. Then he points to the dark spot on the sonogram photos that is the nodule. He says he will need to do another digital examination and on the basis of that, may recommend a biopsy. I go to the table, drop my pants, and bend over again. He pulls on a rubber glove, does the exam with his fingers, and goes back to his little desk.

"*Si necesitaremos una biopsia*," he says—we will need a biopsy. It is not clear to me whether he has actually felt the nodule or the whole prostate, or whether the prostate is enlarged. I have to pee, which I do in the tiny toilet area of his office.

Now Dr. Fernandez launches into the stages I will need to go through with what he is assuming is prostate cancer. He talks about the fact that I may be left *impotente*—impotent—(but maybe not) and *incontinente*—incontinent—(but maybe not). He describes various procedures based on the severity of the problem. But first, the biopsy. He says with a faint smile that it is better to have one done in Mexico, because in the United States, no anesthesia is used. As if we needed one, this nutty piece of misinformation is another indication that the Mexican doctor is somewhat chauvinistic about medicine in Mexico, betraying a troubling insecurity. If I need to go under the knife eventually, I am thinking, will the slightly bigoted Dr. Fernandez be wielding it?

On the way home, Mike and I are silent for long stretches of the drive. It seems inevitable that will have to go through the misery of a prostatectomy. But when...and where? But first, as Dr. Fernandez says, the biopsy. Again, when and where? Later, when we finally talk, I tell Mike I will check about having a biopsy done in Celaya. Meanwhile, I say, I want to check all this with our doctor friend, Marc, in Dallas. I will phone him tomorrow.

Finally Mike speaks. "Fernandez would like nothing better than to cut a prostate from a homosexual man," he says in a chilly tone.

༄

When I left monastic life at twenty-six, my sexual appetite was voracious. But I was also confused about the world of sex, being an innocent. I chose to take up with a girl who was eight years younger than I, but the same age as my sexual self—which had stopped aging and growing the moment I entered the monastery.

Chapter Sixteen

My sexual confusion was so great, and my yearning for exploration so compelling that I leapt at every opportunity to express my sexual self. I brought to this enterprise no sense of personal responsibility and no belief system of self-protection for I was operating outside the religion of my childhood, outside my monastic training, outside all the rules. And, truth be told, I was running faster to catch up with my contemporaries. I was an outlaw, and I approached my life with an outlaw's recklessness.

I was leading a perilous double life: the life on the surface was as a maturing man, rather affable, working through the difficult adjustment from religious to secular life; below the surface and at night I was a prowler after pleasures—the pleasures of the body that I had denied myself for so long, that I had sacrificed on the altar of my youth.

Young men were particularly easy prey, and they suited me well as sexual partners on many counts. First, they were, like me, coming into sexual awareness. They were, like me, crotch-centered and virtually insatiable. Young men and I had much in common, not just in physiology, but in the whole realm of curiosity and desire. Finally, to be with young men meant that I would not be with women, who presented the huge challenge of connecting. To be with a youth was safe and comfortable. Furthermore, I wanted to be with young men because I had never really been one. My late adolescence had been shut down at the gates of the cloister.

And so I found myself roaming the streets at night, picking up young men, and bringing them back to my house. This was easy to do at that time. Bored boys were plentiful in that university town— boys in from the farm, boys starting out at the university and away from home for the first time, boys killing time while waiting for the military to scoop them up and send them to war. I may have been on the prowl for my eighteen-year-old self. And I was finding him in a string of casual nocturnal alliances that only a year earlier would have appalled me. I can still remember their faces and their bodies, some of them.

Whatever I was looking for in those slender young men, I was not finding. It was still outside of me, in them. So "it" would always forever be unobtainable. I was fascinated by their youth, by their charged sexuality, and by their careless masculinity. I loved it. It was how and who I wanted so desperately to be, but damaged as I was by an intervening experience that had shaped my inner life far in advance of my outer life, I felt I could never "be" that. I could only be with it, touch it, worship it, and surrender myself wholly to its mesmerizing charms. These were the sacred offerings to my unquenchable sexual fire. And yet, I was their victim, too, for I solicited them for pleasure, gave them pleasure, and found a momentary joy—if it can be called that—watching them in the throes of their pleasure. I was their servant.

I kept this life secret. I had wanted to chum with these boys, to go with them on their escapades, to get drunk with them, go whoring with them, be rebellious with them. But I realized that on a very basic level I could not. I was in my late twenties now, far removed from the fledgling teen years of the boys I observed with such electrified delight. I settled for holding them in my bed in the night. This was more than compensation for not running with them.

This style of secret life was not without its dangers. Late one afternoon I drove by the spot where I had picked up so many boys and saw a very handsome young man—features of a great beauty. Short brown hair, a wonderful smile, and the perfect body of a young god. He was almost too perfect, in fact. I should have listened to my intuition about him, but his beauty overcame me.

I asked him if he needed a ride, he said he did, and we went to my house. But as we were getting out of the car, he suggested we go to a nearby wooded area because he enjoyed being outdoors—implying that he liked having sex out in the open. I thought this was not a good idea, but he smiled and insisted. We went.

We left the car on the edge of a small woods near a stream. As we sat down on a rock in the shade, suddenly several boys jumped out of the woods, ganged up on me, and began to beat me. I suffered blows to my stomach and my face. They slapped me hard. I fell on the ground and they kicked me. This went on for several minutes while the boys—perhaps six of them—taunted me with names: "What were you gonna do with our friend, Queer?" "Hey, Queer, what were you gonna do? Were you gonna put your dirty queer mouth on his dick?" I did not lose consciousness, but I was on the ground, my face in gravel, with the toughest of the boys straddling me, holding my right arm back. Pain was everywhere in my body, but what I felt mostly was fear. I was bleeding from somewhere on my head or face, and the blood was running into my eyes.

Finally, they had had their fun. One of the boys said that they should get out of there before someone came and saw them. Another boy said, "I have to piss," and the boy who was holding me to the ground said, "Piss on the Queer."

There were other dangerous encounters, but I took the risk for the thrill of the pleasures I stole from them.

Chapter Seventeen

Five Years Before

That winter we went to New Zealand to be present at Mike's brother's wedding. Billy, sixteen months Mike's senior, was marrying a pretty Kiwi girl, Fiona, and we were to be in the wedding party. Mike was the Best Man, I was the Groomsman. In the symmetry to the choices—on the bride's side, Fiona's lovely younger sister was the Maid of Honor, her best friend was the Bridesmaid—we sensed the hand of Mike's mother, or maybe the two mothers together.

Neither Mike nor I had been this far away from home ever. New Zealand, with its stunning natural beauty and its quaint ways—which seemed to us like a throwback to the innocent 1950s in the States—delighted us.

This was the first time, as well, that we had appeared so publicly together as a couple. Standing at the altar in our tuxedoes, spruced up with stiff collars and white carnation boutonnières in our lapels, we had entered into a social convention without apology or shame, and this in a fairly conservative and tradition-bound culture. We were accepted and acceptable, even to the minister and his local congregation, who were perhaps more broadminded than we had anticipated.

This sense of the normal-ness of who and what we were was affirming to both Mike and me—to me, having grown up at a time in our own country when homosexuality was a dreaded secret and a disease, more than him.

As the drama of the wedding ceremony unfolded, I found myself imagining what it would be like to be marrying Mike. Would such a thing look ridiculous? Would it even be possible? And if so, where? Is it something we really wanted, or was it just another way, a pathetic way at that, to copycat conventional heterosexual culture?

I left New Zealand feeling liberated, freer to be myself than I ever had been. Coming home to Mexico, it occurred to me that at least some of my motivation for moving to another country had been the opportunity of reinventing myself as my true self, without hiding behind a large construct of enigmas and excuses. Mike must have noticed this change in me, because he was more demonstrably affectionate with me in public, holding hands briefly while walking down the street, slinging his arm over my shoulder in a restaurant, not fearing that I would recoil or object.

Back in our apartment above Manuel's house, I reflected that I had been living an open life as a homosexual since we arrived in Mexico. For me—and for Mike, too—Mexico had begun to symbolize a refreshingly open way of living. This in spite of the rather narrow, church-bound attitudes in much of Mexican society, especially in our small mountain town. But we were outsiders here, with outsiders' prerogatives. Months before, when we were getting ready to move into Manuel's, he told Mike he would pull a second bed out of his *bodega* for us. Mike said we would not need another bed. Manuel just looked at him for a moment, digesting the situation, as Belen would do a few weeks later, then shrugged and said, "Whatever you prefer is fine with me," referring both to the beds and our sexuality—and, I suppose, the idea of an older man sleeping with a much younger man. We were gringos, not Mexicans, and therefore not bound to the mores of this place.

Gradually, as the months sped by, we met and befriended other same-sex couples, both men and women, and added them to our circle of close associations, most of them heterosexual. The freedom I felt to be living at last a life of total honesty with a partner who was equally open and honest tasted sweet.

༄

Thursday, January 10

I walk to the *farmacia* down the street from our house to refill the antibiotic and I am surprised that the price for twenty pills is the peso equivalent of nearly seventy dollars. It occurs to me that this medical problem threatens to cost me not only stress, but money as well. Later, at the office, I call Marc and tell him about my tests and my visits to the urologist. He is silent for a moment, as if he is mulling the situation over.

"The PSA reading is quite high," he says in a low voice. "It would seem to indicate the presence of malignancy, so you should be prepared for that. Naturally, there is always a chance the nodule could be benign. But...well, the reading is high."

Marc agrees that a biopsy is the next step and says I should consider coming up to the States for treatment; if it is cancerous, I could have the operation to remove the prostate there. For a brief moment, I detect in Marc's mention of going to the States an echo, however faint, of Dr. Fernandez's prejudice in favor of Mexican medicine. The difference, of course, is that Marc is right: medical care for this probably would be better north of the border.

At night, I write a quick email to our friend Luci in Dallas. She has made two retreats with us in San Miguel and we have become friends over the years. Luci, who has beauty-queen looks, was born in Mexico but has lived in the United States most of her life; her husband Ken is a famous surgeon who headed the team that, in 2003, separated the Egyptian Siamese twins who were born joined at the top of the head.

In the letter, I ask Luci if she can recommend a good urologist at the Medical Center in San Antonio.

She must be sitting at her computer, because her reply comes in less than five minutes after I have sent it.

"We don't know of anyone in particular, but we encourage you to take care of this right away. Don't delay. Love, Luci." As the wife of a surgeon, I had expected nothing less urgent from her—as a devoted friend, nothing less tender.

I see you in another life at my side, in Roman times. Yes, you were a runner. I see you coming to me after the race, flushed, smiling with accomplishment, your tunic soaked with sweat, your head wreathed with laurel, your eyes dancing with delight, breathing heavy from the race. I embrace you. You are not blood with me; you are something less—and more. I am older than you. We walk through temple colonnades, down crowded streets, the Via Gulia, the Via Sacra, to the portico of the Curia. I see you lingering with me in the afternoon at the side of a pond, watching fish, watching a swan.

You speak and the words are unfamiliar—what are you saying? Who are you? How have we met here? Where are you going? Do you love me as much as I love you? For, lions tear at my heart when I see you there against that pillar, leaning with your head toward that fountain with the small statue of Neptune in the middle surrounded by water nymphs. I see you and my heart goes wild, yes torn to pieces by the same wild beasts we saw in the arena yesterday feasting on prisoners from Ethiopia—their black flesh disgorging blood the same color as ours, but only seeming darker against their bodies. Some of it splashed on your toga— remember? And I waited for you to be sick, as you had been sick before attending gladiatorial contests with me.

I love you, I say, and you smile back at me, only momentarily stilling the gnawing beasts at the door of my breast. Only for a moment am I safe, truly safe, because I know how fleeting are the thoughts of youth—how ephemeral, like clouds speeding by overhead.

༄

Friday, January 11

Late on this Friday afternoon, perhaps hoping that the clinic staff is gone for the weekend, I call Celaya and ask about a biopsy. One of the staff, a woman, is still at the office. I find out that the clinic there does biopsies on only Monday and Saturday. For me to have one, it will be necessary to go Celaya the night before and get a hotel room, then appear at the clinic very early in the morning. I will need to do an enema two hours before the biopsy. It will cost in the neighborhood of seven or eight hundred dollars. I feel exhausted and discouraged. This black spot on a black-and-white photograph is piling up a mounting series of problems I need to attend to.

In my mind, I am preparing for a laborious project to salvage my health, and not liking any of it.

Saturday, January 12

"I don't want to do anything or talk about anything around this prostate business until Monday," I tell Mike. "Let's just have today and Sunday…let's just have these two days, you know."

"Okay," he says, though I know he does not do well with the feeling of being in limbo. But I need time to digest all this information. So we agree to a moratorium.

Mike phones his parents in San Antonio and tells them that we might have to go up to the States, and asks if we can stay with them while I have the biopsy and, probably, the operation. Bill and Sharron are on their way out of town, but they are supportive and sympathetic, offering their home for anything we might need.

You rise from the grass where we have been sitting with a scroll of Catullus, and brush off your tunic. You put a riddle to me: What is the one thing in Rome that is at the same time ages old and entirely new today? *I think about it for a few moments, but, although I try to stretch my imagination to reach yours, I surrender to you.* The Tiber! *you say, pointing at the slow-drifting river at the edge of the hillside meadow where we have been picnicking and taking our rest. I frown, puzzled.* The Tiber—for it is as old as time, and yet its water came in this very morning! *I laugh with you. You fall to the ground again and pretend to wrestle with me, delighted at your victory.*

Chapter Eighteen

The first time I visited Rome in this lifetime, in my late thirties, I was in a taxi going from Termini Station to my hotel in the Via Aurelia behind the Vatican. I remember feeling confused and turned around. Some of the familiar streets had disappeared and other streets had appeared where none had been. The cypresses that had lined the front of the baths like a spiked honor guard were gone—the baths were gone. A squat building with awnings over the windows now sat in the place where horses were kept. Horses! I had been here before in my long soul's history, perhaps a dozen times, and now I was having difficulty adjusting to the changes that had taken place down the centuries. The eternal city surely was eternal for me.

And Rome seemed to be calling us. Wanting to be closer to the LifePath offices, where Mike did his massage therapy and body work, and I saw clients for counseling, we left Manuel's house and moved into

Centro, to an apartment in a three hundred-year-old building above a coffee shop and bakery half a block from the *Jardin*. The apartment had enormously high ceilings, thick walls, arches, tall windows, and a French door that opened onto a small patio where we kept pots of red geraniums and a table with a huge umbrella. The floors, checkerboard blocks of marble-looking tile in black and butterscotch; long lace drapes, and antique armoires added to the European style of the place. We could have been in the heart of old Rome.

Italy was very much on our minds that spring. For years, since I met him, I had wanted to go to Italy with Mike to show him my ancestral homeland. My grandparents had emigrated from Naples and Sicily to the United States and the little town of Ashtabula, tucked into the northeast corner of Ohio on Lake Erie, in 1904 and 1907. I grew up in the Italian section of town, a section known, actually, as "Swedtown," because Swedish immigrants had preceded by half a century the wave of Italian transplants who eventually settled in and worked at the docks and the railroads.

The Italians brought with them their way of life and superimposed it on this verdant piece of the New World, making it their own. Walking the mile to school every day, I would pass clapboard houses with vegetable gardens in the long backyards, outdoor ovens for baking bread, sometimes a tethered goat or a milk cow. In the mornings I saw women hanging laundry out to dry on lines strung between tall maple trees; in the afternoons, on the way home from school, I saw them unpinning their families' clothes and folding them into huge wicker baskets.

In the summer, I helped my Neapolitan grandmother "turn the tomatoes"—thin slices of ripe Roma tomatoes she had set out on cheesecloth beds attached to curtain-stretcher frames to dry in the sun; my job was to turn the tomatoes over when they had dried out on one side, and then turn them again until they had shrunk to rubbery, burnt-sienna rounds no larger than fifty-cent pieces. In winter, I helped my grandfather cap bottles when his wine was finally ready to leave the wood barrels where it had been sleeping for months in the cool, dark basement.

All the neighbors up and down the street where I lived were Italian, many of them related to me or to each other; all the streets in Swedtown, from the river north to the Lake, were filled with Italian family homes and their gardens and empty lots that were pastures for domestic animals. The spine of Swedtown was Columbus Avenue—named long before Italian immigrants got there, but singularly appropriate after their arrival, since it honored the man who was not only the first American, but the first Italian-American.

The hubs of social life were Our Lady of Mt. Carmel Church, at the intersection of Columbus Avenue and East 16th Street; the grand Sons of Italy Lodge, the red-brick standard issue 1920s Pacific Street Grade School and, a street away, the nearly identical looking Columbus Junior High School; the Young Men's Social Club and East Ashtabula

Club, after-work neighborhood beer joints; Celetti's grocery across the street from the Church; and Candela's sundry store on the opposite corner. The old ones of my grandparents' generation spoke little or no English, so Italian in many dialects was heard everywhere on the streets and in the stores.

In July, on the Feast of Our Lady of Mt. Carmel, the life-sized statue of the saint, with ribbons cascading down her brown and cream robes, was carried through the streets of Swedtown in solemn procession by men of the parish wearing white shirts and black ties and black pants. They stopped at every few houses and set the statue down to allow families to reach up and pin dollar-bills to the ribbons. When the statue reached the corner of Harbor Avenue and East 16th Street, a little girl dressed as an angel, fitted with a heavy leather harness underneath, was hoisted up to a line strung between two telephone poles. She floated across the intersection on pulleys and cables manned by devout stevedores and sang "Gran Signora" while tossing rose petals down on the statue and the crowd.

Gran Signora della terra, vero sol del paradise
Vogli a noi redente il viso, nell 'esilio del dolo…

Now, a hundred years later after my grandparents left Italy, I returned once again, this time with Mike at my side. We decided to make our own grand tour of the highlights: Rome, Florence, Venice, with side-trips to Assisi, Padova, Pisa, and a few other little towns. The photographs we took of each other in those places show us with happy, impish expressions. In one, the first picture I snapped of Mike in Rome, he has just seen the Coliseum and turns to me with his arms up in the air, his face lit up by surprise and delight. In Florence, he is on the Ponte Vecchio in the golden glow of a late afternoon in spring, his face in the close-up soft, composed, inscrutable; he had turned slightly away to watch a child of one of the vendors drop a small stone into the Arno. On a grassy patch under a chestnut tree in a park in Vicenza, he is stretched out leaning on an elbow, nibbling on olives; the sun has come out after a sprinkle.

He took a photo of me in the bustling Mercato San Lorenzo in Florence. I am sitting outside a coffee shop wearing my new black leather jacket, bought earlier that morning in the stalls outside the Medici Chapel, sipping an espresso. Behind me is a mural of this same coffee shop with a throng of people, the owner's friends and family, sitting and enjoying coffee. My face is opened up in amusement, my eyebrows arched up, my espresso lifted in *buon salute*. The picture I took of Mike across the table at the same place shows him lowering his espresso cup after just having tasted for the first time a *café correcto*—a coffee that has been "corrected" by adding alcohol to it, in this case an ample shot of brandy. His look is one of slow, pleasurable revelation, as the drink burned down into his chest, warming him from within.

A few days before that, the afternoon we arrived in Florence on the train from Rome, I got to see a side of Mike I had not known before. As the train pulled in to the Santa Maria Novella station, we gathered up our bags and started moving down the aisle to the door of the crowded car. I led the way with Mike just behind me, but nearing the door he let a woman go in front of him, cutting himself off from me. I had been in and out of Santa Maria Novella probably fifty times over the years—when I spent two months in Florence in the 1980s, the station was my home-base for traveling to other parts of Italy—so I was completely familiar with where things were.

I stepped down from the train and immediately, by habit, turned to the right and started down the platform toward the main concourse. Mike, having lost me, turned to the left. After a minute or so I turned back to see if he was still behind me. He was not there. I began to trace my steps back, pushing my way through the swarm of disembarking passengers. There he was, three cars down, his suitcase in one hand and his backpack in the other, looking stranded and panicky.

"I thought you were right behind me!" I shouted over the sound of the train pulling out on the next track.

Mike did not say anything. It was as if his voice was stuck in his throat. His eyes were full of fear and anger. His face had gone pale.

"Where were you?" he finally managed to blurt out. "I couldn't find you! Don't *ever* do that again. Don't *ever* do that again, do you hear?" He was shaking.

I dropped my bags and reached out to hold him. "It's okay, it's okay." These were the words I used to help calm him when he had his seizure. Now, seeing him like this, I thought he might be on the verge of another epileptic episode here in the station, in the confusion of the crowd with the noise from the trains all around.

I held him close to me as passengers streamed around us. They might have thought we were saying good-bye or hello in the demonstrative Italian way. In a few moments, he was breathing normally again and color had returned to his cheeks.

"I'm so sorry. I promise I will never leave you like that again," I said. "I will never leave you alone like that again."

"You do that, you know. You disappear and I can't find you." Even though the moment of fright had passed, he was still angry with me. Slowly, we started walking down the platform toward the station.

"I promise I won't disappear again," I said, wondering briefly what he meant by that. Do I disappear, I asked myself? If so, how do I do that? Even when I am present, am I somehow not present? My mind sped back to that first morning-after in Las Vegas when Mike was nowhere to be found. "I was hiding," he had said. And I remembered the near-panic I had felt, the loss, the terrible absence.

Have we been hiding from each other down the ages through life after life? Are we playing hide-and-seek with each other, children souls that we are? I know as I live and breathe in this body that we will be together again. Our eyes will connect and our hands will touch. Then our lips will find the lips of the other, and a rush of tenderness will overcome us.

An hour later we had dropped our luggage off at our bed-and-breakfast near the Duomo—a room with a view!—and were ambling through the old streets of Renaissance Florence on our way to the Piazza della Signoria, happy and carefree as children. But the incident at the train station made a lasting impression on me. I had always been afraid that he would leave me. Now, in a sudden flood of discovery, I realized that Mike may have been troubled by the possibility of me abandoning him.

As we looked up at the Perseus of Benvenuto Cellini in front of the Palazzo Vecchio, the hero holding up the trophy of his courageously undertaken adventure, the head of the Medusa, I took Mike's hand and squeezed it lovingly. The forging of the bronze Perseus took Cellini innumerable tries over nearly ten years and bankrupted him; in the final casting, he had his household furniture thrown into the fire to assure enough heat, and the right kind of heat, to make the statue. I wanted to be present with that intensity, truly present, in Mike's life now and always.

Here is a photo of you in Padova in front of the huge Basilica of Saint Anthony, with its Romanesque façade and half-onion shaped domes, your long hair flying in the May breeze. Inside the church we saw the reliquary containing the jaw of the saint, famous for his passionate sermons. Many years earlier I had knelt and prayed here at this tomb of Saint Anthony, patron of lost objects, to find me a companion. I promised the saint that if he would find me the young man of my dreams, I would return to this spot with him. Now I have him in you, and now have returned in gratitude.

Young Stefano comes right up to me at the train station in Padova and says in heavily accented English, "Would you like a drink?" I order a cappuccino and he an acqua minerale *and as we sit at the café table half-grinning at each other he pets my leg. He is twenty-seven, just half my age, but he likes older men. "Your face," he says, and he hesitates—"Come è bello." I take the compliment. The day before, I went to the temple of Saint Anthony. I touched the tomb where his bones have been turning to dust since the thirteenth century and I prayed to the saint who finds things to find me a companion. And here is young Stefano, who when he takes his clothes off in my hotel room is a young god. And still I am not completely excited. He is entranced with the hair on my chest. "Your cock is so big," he murmurs, handing me his own hunk of meat, so silky and so swollen. At the height of our play he says, "go" instead of "come"—"Are you ready to go?" he pants. "Sì," I say.*

I take him back to the train station in the rain and give him my address, which he has asked for. Beyond all the name-brand fashionable clothes, the Gucci shoes, the Calvin Klein briefs—what do I remember? His face, the shortness and curliness of his hair, so short-cropped on his shapely head. Stefano. The saint with the silver tongue has found me a trick who likes me. He says, "I like you" over and over. In the nearby Cappella degli Scrovegni *the panel of Giotto that depicts the kiss of Judas in the Garden of Gethsemane: Jesus looks straight at him, as if to say "Is this love or hate? Is this the comfort I have denied myself so long, unable to connect, unwilling to engage, or are you the betrayer I have waited for in the secret shadows, in the dark corner of my self-loathing? Why have you come? Where are you taking me?"*

Chapter Nineteen

Sunday, January 13

To get out of town and out of our heads, we drive sixty kilometers to Celaya on a shopping trip to Costco and Home Depot, neither of which big stores are in San Miguel. We are almost in Celaya when the car breaks down. A fan belt has broken. We call our mechanic, Julio Cesar, on Mike's cell phone and he tells us he will drive from San Miguel to help us. At first we protest, then we accept his generosity; he is giving up his Sunday afternoon for us. We leave the car at a Pemex, one of the nationalized Mexican gas stations, take a taxi to a shopping center, and eat at a Mexican buffet. I pick at a salad; Mike, really enjoying the stews and chili dishes, goes back to the buffet table three times.

Afterwards, we taxi back to the gas station to meet the mechanic and we all drive to the local Auto-Zone for a belt. Julio Cesar, unlike his can-do namesake from Roman history, is not able to do much—he half-fixes the problem. The other half will be done on Tuesday, because he will need to take the radiator out at his shop. But at least the car, with a new belt, can be driven, if slowly and carefully.

Because the car episode has taken up the entire afternoon, we end up not shopping. We turn around and head back to San Miguel. I take this as a kind of sign, but do not know exactly of what. Maybe the car is like my body, broken and in need of repair. Maybe the unpredictability and undependability of the car is like me and maybe the time it has taken for us to deal with the car is like all the precious days we have spent preoccupied with my prostate gland.

All day, we have not spoken about the situation. Then, on the way back to San Miguel, Mike says, "I know we agreed not to talk about this, but I just want you to know that I will support anything you want to do."

"I know," I say. For the rest of the ride home, we are silent. I keep my hand on his leg and try to swallow back a lump in my throat the whole time.

༄

Four Years Before

We returned to San Miguel bathed in the golden afterglow of Italy. Some months later Mike's parents arrived from Minneapolis and announced that Bill was taking a military judge position in San Antonio, Texas—the closest big American city to our area of Mexico. They wanted to be done with the bitterly cold winter weather and they wanted to live nearer to us. Thus began a round of road-trips over the next few years, with us driving up to San Antonio to visit them and shop, and them driving down to be with us and enjoy the gentle, colorful culture of our adopted country.

I welcomed this inclusion in Mike's family—in fact, I craved it. My own family, what was left of it, was not much of a comfort. I was to fault for that, because I had always distanced myself in order to keep the secret of my sexual preference from them. My mother died at the early age of sixty-four of liver cancer, my father died almost twenty years later, the year before I met Mike. There was a time when I desperately wanted to tell my mother my secret, but the opportunity never seemed to arise. Once, when the subject of girlfriends came up, as it invariably did every time I visited home—"Do you have a girlfriend?" "Oh yes, a bunch, but no one special, Mama." "A bunch…my, my."—I started to say, "Actually, I prefer to be with…" but the words stuck in my throat, dried up, and evaporated into the air like the steam from our coffee cups.

I had a better chance to reveal myself to my father. When my mother, upon whom he had been entirely dependent, died, he was depressed and in a fog, and began to drink. I moved back home from Santa Fe to be with him. About three months later, emotionally back on his feet, he complained to me that he needed a woman and divulged something startling about his sex life with my mother: "She wouldn't let me touch her for years," he said with a mixture of sadness and bitterness.

He found his way into a network of men his age, widowers who were hungry for sex and were prowling around looking for it. There was a woman who serviced these fellows, apparently for a money tip or gifts, like a couple of bags of groceries. She was in their general age bracket—I imagined her with false teeth, since my father told me she was "really good" and did "everything, everything," meaning, I supposed, that she gave oral sex. My father told me about her and suggested I go to her "to get rid of some of those juices." I told him it was not for me—hinting that she might have been too old for me—but that he should go to her and enjoy himself. My father seemed disappointed, but only shrugged and did not bring it up again.

At sixty-six, he surprised my brother and me by taking a girlfriend and moving her into the house. I returned to Santa Fe, having played the dutiful son for nine months. For years after that—I forget how many, six? seven?—I stayed away from Ohio. Now that he had a live-in companion, I reasoned, he did not need me so much in his life. But the real reason I absented myself had more to do with the pain of revealing myself. In my little hometown, in my family, a man in his forties who was not married had some explaining to do; I was not about to put myself through the ordeal of disclosure and become the subject of endless and hurtful gossip.

At some point when my father was still of sound mind and I finally had gone home for a visit, we were sharing a whiskey-and-water, his favorite drink, at the kitchen table, and he suddenly blurted out, "How come you never got married?"

It was the opportunity of a lifetime, but I could not say it, I just could not. What I said was, "Daddy, I guess I'm just not that way."

He nodded, trying to make some sense of what I might have meant. I honestly believed homosexuality was outside of his worldview. When I was growing up, I overheard him say someone was queer, but it turned out to be "peculiar" he had meant, because the epitaph had been levied upon a grizzled old man in the neighborhood who collected rags. I let my chance pass again, although this time I had at least been more determined to reveal myself—and did not lie.

Ten years after my father died I saw him and heard him on a videotape my brother made of him around 1991, six years before his death and a year before he began to sink into senility. By that time he was so hard-of-hearing as to be nearly deaf. My brother had to repeat every question several times. But when my father finally did get the words of the questions, his face lit up and he launched into replies that included stories from family history that stretched back almost a century to another world. He gave first-hand accounts of growing up in Ashtabula Harbor during the Great Depression—how he and his brother Charlie would steal down to the railroad yards on bitter winter nights and pick up chunks of coal that had spilled out of coal cars, stuff them in sacks, and drag the sacks home for the family's furnace; how he saved another boy from drowning one summer afternoon while they were racing back to shore from the break-wall at the Lake; how his brother Anthony, the playmate and buddy of his boyhood, fell out of a tree and a few days later died of his injuries.

My brother sent the video interview to me as a present, but I never looked at it. I packed and unpacked it in cardboard boxes it with books in several places where I lived over the years. One time, while culling my library during a move, I actually considered tossing it out. Why I had waited for more than a decade to watch it is still a mystery to me. Maybe I was putting off some great upwelling that such a face-to-face confrontation with him was bound to produce in me. Maybe I would hear him express his disappointment with me, never having given him grandchildren, never having brought a young daughter-in-law into the family. Would his face show faint scorn when my name came up? It was shame, of course, that kept me from looking at the tape.

When I did at last dust off the plastic case and put the cassette into the machine, I braced myself for an emotional ambush, the revealing of something I had not known before. I watched mesmerized as my brother and my father, both now dead, talked to each other fifteen years earlier at the kitchen table in the old house, the house I had grown up in, about family history. The ambush came three-quarters of the way through when my brother suddenly began asking him whether he and I had been "good kids."

"Oh, very good, very well-behaved," my father said. Then he looked into the eye of the camera, and, it seemed, into my eyes and into my soul. "Of course, Joey was a…a mama's-boy, you know." I stared back into his electronically rendered eyes feeling my heart begin to race. A second later, maybe realizing what he had said and not wanting to go farther down that path, he returned in a lower voice to his former thought: "You were both good kids, good kids."

A mama's-boy. He had known.

༄

Monday, January 14

On Monday morning at the office, I ask Beverly to be with me on a call to Marc. "In case I forget to ask him something," I tell her. But my real reason for wanting her on the phone with me is because I need the support and the comfort. She knows me well enough to know this. Mike is with clients all morning, but even if he were free, I want to make this call without him, maybe to prove that I can do some things without his help. Beverly knows this, as well, and simply, typically, rises to the occasion.

When we get through to Marc, he is with a patient and asks us to call back during lunch. Beverly has to start her work day, so I decide to call him again by myself at noon.

On the phone, Marc tries to be helpful. "You could come here to Dallas—I know a few good urologists," he says. When I ask him about San Antonio, where Mike's parents live, he says there are good urologists at the University of Texas Medical Center. "You could do the biopsy there, then shortly after, the prostatectomy." In his mind, and in mine, there is no doubt I will need to undergo an operation on my diseased prostate. Hopefully, the cancer has not spread to other parts of my body, I am thinking.

In the early evening, Eduardo Morales and Cofe Fiakpui arrive at the house from Tepoztlan, a small town south of Cuernavaca. Eduardo is a contemporary shaman and an expert in polarity and craniosacral therapies. He is in his late forties, with a serene face inherited from his pre-Columbian ancestors. His shaved head seems to emphasize his seriousness as a shaman and healer. Through Beverly, who had studied with Eduardo before I met her, we have been friends for several years, since Mike and I moved to Mexico.

Polarity is a therapeutic method based on the idea that the body is a magnetic energy field, and if the energy centers—*chakras* in Eastern thought—are in balance, well-being results. Craniosacral therapy began in the early part of the last century, a hands-on healing technique in which the practitioner manipulates the cranium with almost imperceptible movements to bring about a sense of deep rest. It can be used to address everything from simple aches and pains to acute and chronic diseases, and even emotional or psychological disorders. Eduardo learned it in Canada. He takes the process a step further into the realm of spiritual healing.

Chapter Nineteen

Over the years Eduardo has worked on me perhaps thirty times. Each time, I could not tell the difference between the two therapeutic approaches; I just zoned out on his massage table after a few minutes, and when he took his hands off the back of my head I slowly returned to the present and he told me what he had "seen." Tonight I am thinking that Eduardo, and Cofe as well, have arrived at exactly the right time for me.

Cofe is a young African-American man—literally: his father is from Ghana, his mother from the United States—who practices a healing modality called Acupoint Kinesiology, which combines energy principles with muscle feedback and reflexes to measure the body's response to stimuli. He adds to this Chinese Herbology, so that after he tests you by placing his fingertips lightly on the backs of your hands and diagnoses a physical problem, he can suggest an herbal treatment to take care of it. Standing a full 6 feet 3 inches, built like an athlete, sporting a head of coal-black curly hair and a black beard, he is an impressive presence. He is utterly dedicated to his path in life: when he first set up his practice, he named his website cofethehealer.com.

In the evening, Cofe goes to the office, four blocks away, to unpack his herbs and prepare his room for the next day. Eduardo and I sit at the table in the kitchen. I tell him what has been going on with me the past month. Even though I am obviously stressed, I am surprised that I can talk about this in an organized, chronological way.

"You've really been through a lot," he says quietly, sympathetically. I can see in his eyes and his manner a subtle shifting from old friend to shaman-healer "Can you show me the test results and the sonogram?"

"Of course," I say, going into my bag for the large manila envelope from the hospital lab and handing it to him. He takes the pictures out first and looks at them carefully. Then he scans the summary of the report.

"Do you know exactly what this says? It's medical Spanish, quite technical, so you may not have gotten the full meaning. This black spot here—it's an abscess, very small, six millimeters." He puts his thumb and forefinger almost together to show me the approximately size.

"But it's a nodule—it could be a tumor," I say. "And it could be malignant." I am feeling the beginning of alarm, thinking that Eduardo may want to minimize the test results to reassure me in some way and relieve my anxiety.

Eduardo stares at me as if he is having one of his shamanic visions. He is looking past me, or looking at my aura, or just looking at me, through me, and mulling something over. Is he seeing my diseased self, or simply my panic—or something else?

"I don't think so," he says after a long silence. "It's an abscess, like a boil. I don't think you're sick. You look healthy to me."

For a moment I feel like a condemned prisoner who has just been told that new evidence has been discovered in his case, the evidence exonerates him, and he is free to walk out of the prison—but, for some reason, does not make a move to leave. Eduardo's explanation helps me a little, but I have been thinking I have cancer of the prostate and that the malignancy may have metastasized to other parts of my body, so this new information, and how I feel about it, is unfamiliar.

Eduardo is tired from the trip. He excuses himself and goes up the stairs to his bedroom on the third floor. I am scheduled to have an appointment with Cofe the next day. I will also have a craniosacral session with Eduardo. Later, getting ready for bed, Mike asks if I have contacted the Medical School in San Antonio to arrange a consult and a biopsy.

"No," I say, and I tell him what Eduardo said about the reports.

"An abscess?" Mike seems skeptical. Such is our combined level of fear at this point that we both are feeling we need to proceed on the path outlined by the doctors.

"Look, whatever comes up in the next couple of days with Eduardo and Cofe, I'll still make an appointment with a doctor at the UT Medical School in San Antonio," I tell him.

"That's good, let's cover the medical base—this is nothing to play around with." Then, as if he is sealing my agreement with him, he kisses me.

"I promise," I say.

Chapter Twenty

There is a photo of you I took in our hotel room on that last morning in Rome just before we left, you sitting with your arm resting on the wide window sill, the window open reflecting the red-tiled roof and mustard-colored wall of the building across the street. The creamy light is full on your face, you are turned toward it and staring out, as if trying to see beyond the present into the future. What will your life be like after I am gone? How will you remember me? When you take that other inevitable lover in your arms, will you recall the scent of my body, how my skin felt to your tender touch, how you nestled your head in the warm crook of my neck, how you used to rest your hand between my thighs before you drifted off to sleep?

Was it in Rome I first thought we might have been together in other lifetimes? From the moment we arrived there by car from the airport I felt it. Do you remember the driver, that grave patrician presence with the sharp prominent nose, how he stated proudly, almost arrogantly, when I asked him if he was born in Rome, "Si, sono Romano…"?

I am Roman, too, I thought, as if it was a palpable truth. And my lover here by my side, as well, Romans all.

If we have been together before, will we be together again in some distant land, in some distant time? How will I recognize you? Will we be lovers again?

How will we hear the call to love in the pipes of the goat-god Pan next time?

༄

Tuesday, January 15—Morning

In the sala of our retreat center, I have a session with Cofe. His healing method, based on reading energy, requires a bare room with white walls, so the room is empty, except for a table covered with a white blanket, two chairs and a low bench. Metal will ruin the sensitive energy readings, which is why we sit on wood chairs and have removed coins from our pockets and rings from our fingers. In a corner of the room three small tables set in an L shape hold what looks like a hundred or more white plastic bottles of Chinese herbs.

I sit across from him on one of the chairs and rest one arm on the table, on which there are a number of tiny glass bottles containing "witnesses," energetic samples of various viruses, bacteria, and other microorganisms. Cofe touches the back of my hand with his fingertip, then joins the forefingers and thumbs of both his hands in a chain link. If the chain breaks quickly, it means something; if it holds, it means something else. He repeats this thirty or forty times to get readings. On the basis of his findings, he mixes up a compound of herbs to address the problem.

I have been seeing Cofe once a month for over a year. Last year, he brought me back to health from Hepatitis-B, which had sent me to bed for a month. Today, he is complaining that he is not getting good readings.

"Do you have any metal in your pockets?" he asks. "Belt buckle? Change?"

"No, nothing."

He still cannot get good energy signals—his fingers break when they should not, they hold at the wrong times. Now he looks down, rolls his eyes, and sighs deeply. In his haste to get to the office this morning, he has forgotten to remove a metal necklace he wears when he is not working. He sighs and whips it off, tosses it into a straw basket on a far table. But something else is flawing his readings. He moves two large boxes of herbs from one corner of the room to another, farther away, because the energy of the herbs might be jinxing the analysis. By now, our time has run out and we reschedule for tomorrow. I am thinking that my prostate problem may be one that Cofe cannot help.

When I return to my office, I find it hard to concentrate. What if Cofe was getting good readings but did not want to tell me the bad news? What if my condition itself was interfering somehow with the readings, throwing them off because of the rapid spread of the cancer?

How proud I was of you that day! I beamed with the pleasure of that exhilarating moment: you receiving your Bachelor of Science degree in Natural Health. You did it all so diligently. As I sat at the party celebrating your accomplishment, chatting with the guests at our retreat center, my mind went back to the times I would find you immersed in a book or writing in one of your test manuals. I so admired your ability to focus, to concentrate, to be thorough. When I would see you like that, hunched over on the couch in child's pose deep into an engrossing chapter, my love for you blazed up. I knew I could never be as methodical as you. I would have rushed through those books, those tests; I would have read the tests first, then gone back to find the answers in the books. I would have cut corners and made do.

Echoes come to me from past places, of you completing a race, passing a test, overcoming an obstacle—and me at the other end holding my arms out to receive you triumphant. You are a runner, your body is oiled for the contest, your hair a mass of black curls held back with a band of wool woven with metal, with thin threads of gold. I embrace you victorious and feel your wildly beating heart against my chest. A garland of small roses wrapped with laurel falls at your feet; you turn and wave at the girl who tossed it from above on the parapet.

Surely we are moving together through the winding tunnels of time, now apart, now joined again, meeting one another around corners, recognizing each other at intersections, surprised and delighted to be side-by-side once more. I reach over in bed in the morning before the first light comes into the room: I put my hand on your warm belly and hold you and pull you more to me. You are here, asleep, alive. I have found you again.

☙

Tuesday, January 15—Afternoon

This afternoon I have a session with Eduardo. When I arrive at his treatment room, which is above my own office at the Center, I try to smile, but Eduardo can tell I am worried and despondent. I lie down on his massage table and his hands go to the back of my neck. He cradles my head, making minute movements on my cranium. In a few moments, I am adrift—not asleep, but in state of deep relaxation, the Alpha-state.

More than an hour has passed, but I am not aware of the time. To me, it seems like a few minutes. Coming slowly into a hazy present, I stare up at Eduardo.

"What did you see?" I ask.

For a moment he is silent, as if he is searching for words to attach to a shamanic vision that has no words.

"What I saw is this—I saw the abscess. And this is what it is: it is your fear of not having enough tenderness and kindness, or of having these things and fearing that you will lose them."

Tenderness and kindness.

In my mind I go immediately to that terrifying moment last summer when Mike and I were between houses, house-sitting for friends. My brother had died three weeks earlier. Both Mike and I were under tremendous stress and not communicating with one another.

That afternoon he accused me of hiding from him, withholding myself from him, and dropping out of our relationship. He thought it might be best if we each went our own ways.

I was devastated at the thought of breaking up: I knew in an instant that if he left me, I would die. During the brief space of our heated conversation I felt something go into my chest, like a dart, and from there sink slowly down to the lowest bottom part of my internal organs.

On Eduardo's massage table, as I recall that devastating afternoon, the awareness dawns in me that my prostate issue—all this about a black spot, a nodule, a biopsy, impotence, incontinence, cancer ending in death—may have started the moment I felt my heart pierced that day. This "prostate thing" may be entirely about my fear of losing Mike, and with him the most tender and kindest love I have ever known.

I rise from the table slowly and walk downstairs and around the retreat center in a bit of a cloud that does not clear.

I do not call San Antonio for a doctor's appointment.

For now, I decide to keep my thoughts to myself and not discuss any of this with Mike. Maybe I am afraid to hope. Tomorrow, I say to myself, after I see Cofe, I will talk to Mike.

Wednesday, January 16

"The black spot on the sonogram...it's a cyst," Cofe says this morning after half an hour of reflexology testing. The black-and-white pictures from the lab are at the far end of the table, looking discarded, useless.

"A cyst?" I ask, trying for a moment to remember what exactly a cyst is.

"Yes, you know, a bump of flesh, like a sore. I think it's not—in fact, I'm a hundred-percent sure it is benign, because it's perfectly round and does not have jagged edges."

I stare at Cofe without blinking, without feeling anything. I notice that his eyes are dark brown, like mine, and his eyebrows are the blackest of black and the consistency of steel wool. He stares back at me with a look that seems to ask if I had heard what he has just said.

"So, a cyst," he repeats.

"I see."

According to his testing, which today is unambiguous and on-target, some weeks or months ago bacteria from my urinary tract lodged itself in my prostate, where it caused an infection and created a cyst. He says he can dissolve the cyst with herbs.

"But the PSA reading..." I say, hearing myself almost protest against his optimistic diagnosis. After all, the doctors said my prostate is in grave danger—and now?

"The PSA reading was high because your immune system overreacted to fight the infection," Cofe says, ignoring my momentary incredulity. With an herbal formula, he can bring the PSA back to near-normal or normal by my next meeting with him a month from now. He suggests that I get another PSA test a week before he returns.

This new take on my condition and Cofe's straightforward, minimal recitation of the testing results, as if he is treating a paper-cut or a stubbed toe, stuns me. I search around for an emotion to cling to.

Cofe fixes me a strong mixture of herbs that includes high-quality saw palmetto, a healer and conditioner for the prostate. I am to take a small spoonful four times a day with warm water. He tells me that I can stop taking Xatral OD, the pill that the urologist gave me to relax the bladder opening so I can pee freely and not have to pee so much. The herbs will address that issue. The herbs will also work synergistically with the Cipro antibiotic. I should continue taking the Cipro until I run out.

Part of me says that this is too easy—like the first comment out of the mouth of Dr. Fernandez: a urinary discomfort brought on by traveling. An hour ago, I had been assuming, even after Eduardo's dramatic connecting of the emotional dots for me yesterday, that I have cancer of the prostate gland, a cancer that may have metastasized to other parts of my body.

I spend the rest of the day thinking over what Cofe has told me. I take the herbs—I do not take the

Xatral—and wait for something to happen. When I go over the session with Mike in his office, his face opens into a big grin.

"I think his analysis is right-on," he says. "See how you feel tomorrow."

By evening, peeing fairly well without the pills, I am feeling hopeful. But, what if Cofe is wrong? Am I being foolish? What if this *is* cancer I am dealing with—and what if delaying medical treatment, real medical treatment, allows the cancer to spread and become fatal?

Chapter Twenty-One

Three Years Before

A letter arrived in the mail inviting me to attend the forty-fifth anniversary of high school graduation. I left it on the dining room table tucked in with some bills and magazines, dismissing it for the moment.

"I see your high school classmates are going to have a reunion," Mike said after he had sorted through the mail later in the day. "Are you going to go?"

"It's always the same people and the same thing—it's boring." I had been to the class reunions every five years for maybe the past twenty years. Our class, around eighty of us from the small Catholic high school in our small town, was a tightly-knit group. Through the years, we had kept in touch with one another either directly or indirectly—and some of us had forged strong life-long friendships with other class members. To this day I write weekly—sometimes three or four times a week—to Mary Lou, who had been my date at the senior prom.

"Maybe we should go together...that would make it a lot less boring," he said, breaking out in a light laugh, suggesting a scene. "Seriously, though, it would be a chance to see where you grew up and to meet your brother."

Meeting my brother, of course, would contain all the aspects of a coming out ritual; the idea at first was wrenching. But it was time.

So, in the first week of August we flew to Cleveland, rented a car and drove up to Ashtabula—"up by Ashtabula," as Jack Kerouac says in *On the Road*, the book he wrote in 1951 when I was nine. When I read it in college in the early 1960s just those three words brought back a rush of warm emotions and a thousand images: sitting under a huge maple tree on the lush grass on the side of my grandparent's house on summer afternoons; riding my bicycle on the uneven, tree root-raised sidewalks of Harbor Avenue, the stringing wind of early spring on my face; kicking up a carpet of orange and yellow and green fall leaves after a rain in front of the nun's house on East 16th Street on the way to school.

And another connection with that book: Neal Cassady, Kerouac's major character under the name Dean Moriarty, died of a drug overdose, apparently, or simple exposure (he was wearing only jeans and a tee-shirt) in February 1968 on the side of the railroad tracks in San Miguel de Allende, Mexico, the town that, thirty years later, would become my home.

Chapter Twenty-One

Mike and I stayed with two of my classmates who had been married since high school, Joe and Mary Kay, a handsome couple who still had the golden aura of class leaders—football hero and homecoming queen—about them. I had thought that appearing with Mike at my side at the alumni reunion dinner would be the big self-revelation event of this trip, but I had somehow forgotten what kind of an impact our appearance might have made on my brother Michael and his wife, and their grown married daughter.

Two years earlier, my niece's husband had won a million dollars on a TV quiz show. They took some of the money and bought our family home from my brother, whose health had begun to decline. Michael had been a policeman for thirty years in our little town. The stresses of the job and the adult-onset diabetes that had killed both my mother and her mother had left him with a weakened heart and barely functioning kidneys and lungs.

When I walked into the house that he and Joyce now called home—a cute and clean tiny place in a retirement subdivision—he was standing at the kitchen counter that separated the kitchen-dining area from the living area, leaning on it, really. The moment he saw me he teared up in what looked to me like a mixture of embarrassment at his alarmingly poor health, grief, loss, helplessness, and joy at my coming to visit him. His skin was dark and jaundiced and blotchy, his hands unnaturally thin and waxy. He had lost weight since I had seen him three years earlier, or it had shifted so that his waist had gone down, but his legs had swollen up. His eyes, dark and shadowed, seemed to say, "Look what's become of me! Who would have thought when we were growing up together, you my older brother by six years, that I would be this sagging bag of sick flesh? I'm going to die...I would rather die than have you see me like this." Looking at him, my heart broke. I enfolded him in my arms and kissed him.

After he had met Mike and we all visited over lunch, Mike and Joyce disappeared into the living room and my brother sat alone together over coffee. I was still adjusting to seeing him so physically devastated. We spent a few minutes chatting about the family, the cousins, what had divorced and remarried, who had died, who was sick. Then he pulled himself a little closer to me across the table and lowered his voice.

"Is this it?" he asked.

My eyebrows went up over a quizzical expression as I waited for him to explain his question.

"Is this it?" he asked again. "I mean, is Mike your...your partner for good, or just, you know, a friend?" I could understand his struggle for words; for many years I had no words to describe my boyfriends, hook-ups, lovers.

"He's my partner—my life-partner. We've been living together for seven years. So, I guess this is it." I smiled briefly, but when he did not smile back I melted back into the seriousness of the moment.

"The reason I'm asking you if this is it—if this is your choice—is I want to know if you are wanting us to accept Mike into the family." I was completely unprepared for this. And yet, this was exactly what I was doing—presenting Mike as a new member of the family, waiting for the approval and acceptance of the only family left to me, my brother, whose flesh and blood were also mine. It suddenly seemed like something out of *The Godfather.* Family, *la famiglia*: for Italians: everything.

"Yes, I suppose I am." I lowered my eyes and stretched out my hand across the table to him. He held my hand. Long moments passed as he petted and patted my hand.

"What took you so long to come out to me?" he asked, using a startling in-the-know expression. I could not lift my eyes.

"I guess I thought you knew," I said finally. When my eyes met his at last, what I saw in his face, so dark and drained, was a mixture of scolding and compassion. He seemed to be thinking, how would things have been different between us all these years if you had been honest with me?

"I didn't know," he said. "We all wondered, of course. But you were always very private about yourself. Naturally, we respected that." He let go my hand gently and picked up his coffee cup. From the other room I heard a burst of laughter from Joyce and Mike, who were looking at old photos in an album.

"I was afraid, I suppose, and ashamed." The words were coming out of my mouth without my planning them or editing them. I must have imagined this confession a hundred times in the far back of my mind.

Michael turned his head aside and coughed into a fistful of wadded up tissues, then faced me again across the table and took a sip of coffee.

"You're my big brother," he said, his eyes glassy, whether from the coughing or the emotion of the moment. "Do you think I would have loved you less if...if you had told me all this a long time ago?"

"No, not at all," I said quickly. "It was hard for me, that's all. It was hard."

Michael nodded. He reached over and patted my hand again. "I think Mike is a good guy. He's our family, now."

We sat there for some time not saying anything. There did not seem to be anything else to say, really. As we lingered over our coffees, looking out the sliding glass back door of the little house into a wooded area, a quiet came over us.

Two years later I would be in the same house sitting at this same table hunched over a cup of coffee, but my brother would be in the guest bedroom a few feet away sitting on a hospital bed in a stupor, filling up with fluids because he had elected to take himself off of dialysis. It was there in the bedroom I would sit with him and hold him and tell him, not knowing if he could hear me, that he was my baby brother and that I loved being his brother all these years and that outside the window a beautiful May afternoon was drifting into early evening and the lilacs had come out on the big bush at the side of the house.

Later that day, the two Mikes spent some time together. My brother told him stories of us growing up. Mike opened up and talked about his own upbringing with his brother. They were alike in many ways—both named Michael, both born under the sign of stubborn and earthy Taurus, now connected in a deeper way, through me, to each other.

After that, the class reunion was somewhat anticlimactic. Mike and I attended the dinner at the Ashtabula Elk's Club, I introduced him to my school friends as my life-partner, we sat and ate dinner at a table for four with my prom date Mary Lou and her husband, Chuck. I suppose there was gossip, but if there was it did not reach my ears. Some of my classmates who I had been close to in high school appeared to be somewhat distant that night, as if they were mulling over how to react to their friend of many years—almost half a century—presenting himself not only as homosexual, but as the lover of a young man thirty years his junior, the age of their own children.

Mostly what I remember about that night was the alarming physical deterioration of these kids I had grown up with. Here was the boy who lived on the same street as me, who I walked to school with every day and, when we were teenagers, played in the school band together, recovering, not well, from quadruple bypass surgery, walking with a cane. Here was the girl who had been one of the star cheerleaders, in a wheelchair struggling from the effects of a botched hip replacement. Here was the girl who had admired the nuns so much, who used to trade secrets about them in Italian with me in the hall between classes, sunken, in remission for the moment from cancer of the colon.

All of them had aged to the point where I had to strain to see in their faces and wiry whitened hair and their often bloated and oddly misshapen bodies the fresh eighteen-year-olds I had known on graduation day so long ago, the week before I left this place forever to join a monastic order and hide my sexuality away from them.

And what of me? Am I not as old as these others? When I look at you, my love, I see youth and somehow by emotional osmosis I think of myself as being your age, not mine. I send a photo of us together in Assisi to a lawyer friend in Santa Fe and he writes back that you and I have begun to look alike. Can that be true? Could I actually become younger by gazing at your young face? But no, I see in the photo my own hair going to silver and my features softening. And that was then. Now, five years later, caught helplessly in time's rushing river, am I not even older looking? How much more time—how little time—is left to me to love you?

The following spring you completed work on your bachelor's degree in Natural Health. How proud of you I was the night we threw a huge party at LifePath Center and entertained a hundred and fifty people in your honor! Belen and her comadres *cooked an enormous comida—enchiladas with red spicy sauce and green* tomatillo *sauce, shredded* pollo, *steaming bowls of black frijoles, Spanish rice,* pico de gallo, *thick blue corn tortillas, guacamole,* ensaladas verdes. *You were the man of the moment. After we gave our little speeches, you acknowledged the support you had gotten from clients and friends by saying that you considered all of us part of your graduating class.*

Chapter Twenty-One

Mike took a couple of weeks off from his studies, then launched into them again, determined to earn his doctorate as soon as possible. The road to becoming a Naturopathic Doctor was a steep one, but he was committed to it. I saw in his enthusiasm for the future a new, sturdier sense of himself as an adult and fell in love with him again, as I had so many times before at these life milestones.

The night of the party I had a dream that I was present at an initiation. I was a priest-mentor in a place like Atlantis, he was my student.

You stood in the middle of the temple at noon and a round skylight opened to reveal the searing sun piercing the dark temple through a special prism in the center of the domed ceiling. The colors were dazzling. There was a rush of excitement in the hall. And then the disk of colored light which fell on your white robe began to turn and churn and expand, refracting against the walls, filling the place with a strange uplifting energy.

Chapter Twenty-Two

The spring before Mike got his degree, I signed a contract for a new book, a spiritual memoir called *God On Your Own: Finding a Spiritual Path Outside Religion*. I spent the rest of that year writing the book. Early the following year, as it was being edited, Mike and I planned a trip to New Mexico to help launch the book in the Southwest. We had not been back to Santa Fe in six years. This would be our opportunity to reconnect with old friends and revisit the places we had known when our relationship was young.

We drove from San Miguel up to San Antonio, where we paid a visit to Mike's parents, then flew to Albuquerque for the first of several bookstore talks and signings in the area. A few days later we went up to Santa Fe, which in early June lay scorched under an unusual extended spell of hot, dry weather. Oddly, although I had lived there for twenty-four years, I had trouble finding my way around Santa Fe. Things seemed changed around—or I had changed. I had spent vastly more time in this town than Mike had, but he seemed to remember it better and ended up leading me around.

It came as a great surprise to me that after a quarter of a century of calling this place my home I should be disoriented and feeling lost in it. I had been away only six years, but so complete was my re-invention of myself in Mexico, apparently, it seemed like a lifetime. I had trouble finding streets and landmarks, and those I found seemed curiously run-down.

The famous Plaza, through which I had walked daily all those years, some days many times, appeared defunct and abandoned. An influential travel magazine had named it, in its heyday only two decades before, "one of the great public spaces in the Americas." Now the grass had yellowed from drought or neglect, the white enamel paint on the fin de siècle cast-iron benches was chipped and dirty and scribbled on with gang graffiti.

In the evening, Country-Western music poured out of tinny speakers on the gazebo to the amusement of families from Oklahoma and West Texas, tots in tow. It was as if the Plaza of old had been replicated on the same spot it had once occupied and turned into an outdoor museum, a small-scale theme park for budget-conscious vacationers from the neighboring states, people who could get here in their SUVs, which had room in the back for baby strollers.

I had come to Santa Fe in the mid-1970s from Los Angeles, where I had been trying, with uneven success, to be a screenwriter. A large part of my decision to leave Hollywood had to do with a calling I felt to do "serious" writing—and the dawning awareness that I was not going to be afforded that opportunity in a place where stories were "pitched" by "concept" and "treatment" merchants. Naturally, I could have been simply avoiding the hard work it surely would have taken to make the interminable rounds of agents, managers, story-editors, producers, and so on with my script ideas. Besides I was a solitary writer, not a collaborative one—group artistic activities always confused me, leaving me frustrated. I wanted to write a novel. When friends relocated to Santa Fe from Manhattan and suggested we share a house, I jumped at the chance.

Snow began to fall the January night I arrived. At dawn I looked out my window on the field across the street, a dazzling ice-blue carpet with clumps of frosted juniper pine here and there and a large, bare-branched weeping mulberry, black against the snow. Having lived for two years in the mild climes of Southern California, and having driven all the previous day through the deserts of Arizona and Western New Mexico, the sight of snow was magical. In the 1920s, during the first flush of coast-to-coast railroad tourism, some member of some Chamber of Commerce of some New Mexican town had named the state "The Land of Enchantment." That first morning in Santa Fe was for me a moment of sheer enchantment that caught and held me for many years, all the years, in fact, of my young adulthood.

Still "undiscovered," the town offered its gems to the newly arrived at bargain prices. I lived in the landmark John Sloan house on Garcia Street, about three blocks from the Plaza, a rustic old adobe with kiva fireplaces and thick-beamed ceilings and the remnants of Dolly Sloan's hollyhock garden in the courtyard. The rent for each of us, when shared three ways, came to around a hundred dollars a month.

Sloan was a New York artist, a member of the Ashcan school of painters whose realistic work in the early part of the twentieth century reflected the grime and grit of urban life. Starting in 1920, when he bought the house I lived in, until 1950, he spent four months of every year well outside of that urban grime and grit among the pristine splendors of Santa Fe where he found himself in time part of a large group of painters who gravitated there over the decade from the East Coast, some for reasons of health (I have never been able to understand how the thin mountain air containing less oxygen than at sea level was considered salubrious for victims of tuberculosis, but...). A tireless worker, he painted every day, and when he tired of his canvases he painted the windows and doors of the house.

During his first Santa Fe summer, Sloan became friends with Will Shuster, recently arrived from Philadelphia, a World War I veteran who had been gassed in France and had sustained injury to his lungs which developed into tuberculosis, and an aspiring painter. Shuster became a diligent student of Sloan. Shuster was a quick study; soon he was making his own excellent paintings, most of them featuring local scenes and characters. One week in the mid-1930s they engaged in a mutual portrait contest—Sloan painting Shuster painting Sloan, Shuster painting Sloan painting Shuster. This artistic duel took place in what would become, many years later, my bedroom.

In 1988 I received a phone call from Don Shuster, Will's son, then in his seventies, asking whether I would be interested in writing a biography of his father. Don was dying of cancer and wanted to leave behind a meaningful legacy, the story of the dad he adored and a sketch of Santa Fe in the period between the wars. He had all of Shuster's diaries, notes, and drawings in ten cardboard boxes in his garage.

The book came out two months after Don died, but before he went to the hospital for what would be the last time, he was able to read the galleys and, one hopes, through them live again a Santa Fe childhood imbued with bohemian abandon, colored by wild weekend-long parties attended by flamboyant heiresses, wildly eccentric artists, and hilarious, heroic alcoholics of both genders.

At the time I went to live there, Santa Fe was not yet recognized as a tourist destination. The big controversy in the local newspaper raged over whether to pave Canyon Road, now one of the art world's most famous streets, lined with bustling studios and galleries and fancy restaurants. The voices raised in favor of paving argued that it would improve the marketing of art to the benefit of artists and property owners, and bring an influx of revenues into the town's meager coffers; those against the paving said it would start Santa Fe down a path of no return toward commercialization and development, which would appeal to the worst elements and destroy the serenity of the old and slow ways of the place, which nearly half a millennium ago had been the quiet, stately backwater capital of Northern New Spain.

There were three or four years at the end of the 1970s when the town actually lived up to its enchanting reputation, earned among a few select visitors over the years, insiders, as a vibrant colony of artists overlaying a unique and rich confluence of three cultures—the Native American Pueblo, the Spanish Colonial, and the American East and Midwest Anglo, an assortment of trappers first, then merchants, then entrepreneurs and land barons. Small, cozy bookstores, all independent in those days, seemed to be everywhere. The coffee was good, the food was cheap, housing affordable, and the people pleasant. The extraordinary beauty of Santa Fe, banked up against the majestic backdrop of the Sangre de Cristo Mountains, magically rose-hued at sunset, was a breathtaking inspiration that seemed to renew itself in every season, at every successive month, in every hour following upon hour, from the sharp slices of sunlight that cut across smooth adobe walls in early morning to the soft gold light at twilight melting over the flat roofs out of which stuck chimneys sending up thin lines of sweet-smelling piñon smoke.

Chapter Twenty-Two

Lilacs bloomed all over town that first spring, billowing up in the dusty alleys behind streets lined with old elms sprouting tender light green leaves, lilac shoots clinging against the stone walls at the side of the cathedral, crowding all over the timeworn adobes along the Acequia Madre—more lilacs than had been seen in many years—giant fragrant blooms of deep purple and violet and white on huge bushes, filling Santa Fe with perfume for nearly a month, so that wherever we went we seemed to be swathed in a fog of floral aromas.

The river ran clean and fast that year from the melting snow on the mountains, down through the little neighborhoods on the north side, down into town under the bridge on the Paseo de Peralta near the cathedral school, down through the historic center alongside the Alameda into the Guadalupe area, down past the barrios to the desert places south of town, oven-hot and parched except for this miraculous rush of cold water. I watched summer sunsets from atop the Cross of the Martyrs, continents of clouds moving gold-edged over the waning sun. At night, the sky above the backyard of the Sloan house was filled with stars that had lowered themselves, it seemed, out of their black velvet settings and hovered so close overhead that I could almost touch them: the swaying shadows of hollyhocks, the sound of crickets on those nights in late summer.

The smell of roasting chiles in the crisp air announced the start of autumn, a long leisurely period before the first snow. The touching, colorful annual Fiesta in September; the aspens cloaking the mountainsides in October, long hikes above the timberline; the chill nights of November filled with the sounds of rasping leaves and after that again the snow, and in the snow *farolitos*, little brown paper bags with votive candles inside lighting paths, piñon *luminarias*, the sweet scent of anise from baking *biscochitos*.

Then in the early 1980s travel magazines began running extravagant full-color spreads on the glories of Santa Fe. The summer tourist population doubled, then tripled. The facilities at the ski basin were upgraded and skiers flocked to Santa Fe, as well, swelling winter tourism. Car and truck traffic increased, and with it, prices. Modest mom-and-pop restaurants serving humble *posole*, enchiladas, and flan suddenly became upscale, offering *oso buco* and radicchio salads and tiny squares of tiramisu on oversized plates. For tourists, lodging and transportation prices soared. An emerging Hispanic middle-class sold their adobe homes on the fashionable East Side out from under their freshly dead grandparents to eager buyers from California and Texas, for whom the ludicrously inflated prices were good deals to be pounced upon.

Each passing month brought quantum changes in the direction of a numbing sameness: national brand retail chain stores like Banana Republic and J. Crew and Eddie Bauer moved in; Woolworth's Five-and-Dime Store, which had been on the Plaza for nearly a century, went out of business; shopping malls sprouted where there once were empty fields filled in summer with wild sunflowers, and

Chapter Twenty-Two

in autumn by clusters of mustard-colored chamisa. Bookstores closed.

But those years just before the boom were good for me. In the months after I arrived I wrote a novel, which was published the next year. *The House of Alarcon* is the story of a Spanish Colonial family in Northern New Mexico and the royal land-grant they lived on and cultivated through several generations and now, in contemporary times, were in danger of losing to an unscrupulous developer. I re-read it after many years when I was touring around the south of Spain on the train and saw in it a premonition of the end of the romance of Santa Fe I must have been sensing when I wrote it.

Now, thirty years after I arrived there for the first time, with only a suitcase stuffed with clothes, three boxes of books, and a manual typewriter, I was back again, this time with my life's partner at my side. Perhaps much of the distance I felt upon reentry had to do with who I was when I lived there and who I was now. My years in Santa Fe were cast over with loneliness and an isolation born of shame. I was hiding out most of the time in my secret sexuality. It was only near the end of my Santa Fe sojourn, when Mike came into my life, that the cloud of unhappiness brought on by aloneness began to lift. By then it was clear that I wanted to reframe my identity completely as a man without shame, in a committed relationship with another man, a much younger man, and required an entirely new place in which to do it.

We took an afternoon off the book tour and drove up to Las Vegas, where we had met eight years before. The coffee bar where I had seen Mike for the first time and fell in love was gone, but the little hotel where we had spent our first night together was still there, looking exactly as it had looked then, without even a change of lace curtains or green shades on the windows. Before returning to Santa Fe, we walked along Bridge Street to the Plaza deep in thought, deeply grateful for having found each other here.

"You've had a whole life without me," Mike said as we sat on a bench in the shady Plaza. The day had been uncomfortably warm, but now in the late afternoon under the trees a breeze came in and there was freshness in the air. A fly buzzed around us.

"And you without me," I said with a smile.

"I want us always to be together now." He pulled my hand over to his thigh and held it there.

Back in Santa Fe we reconnected with old friends—paramount among them our dear Diane—and greatly enjoyed their company, and that made the journey enjoyable for us. We even found ourselves becoming closer to one another, as if the shared experience of recollecting the past had led us up another step in our intimacy. But the town itself was a disappointment: the soul that had animated the place and made it fascinating to me when I was a much younger man had fled, leaving only these endless new tracts of brown houses baking in a brown landscape under a hostile sun, waiting for the water to run out.

Not surprisingly, going back to Santa Fe presented me with another opportunity to contemplate the passing of time. I had gone there as an enthusiastic young man, full of wonder and possibility, full of hopes and plans for the future. Everything I saw was stunning, charmed, exotic, mystical. I returned as an older man complaining about the heat, annoyed at the high prices in the restaurants, impatient with the bumper-to-bumper traffic, critical of the air quality. I was slower getting in and out of cars. I could not remember some people or places.

Am I getting old? Do you see me faltering, forgetting, watching my steps, being extra careful? You tell me that you are concerned about your own hairline, which seems to be receding. I see the pencil-thin creases at the sides of your eyes that you pointed out to me some time ago. We are aging, yes, but we are getting older together. You say to me this is the best time of your life. I agree and say it is by far the best time for me, as well.

Were we here in this wilderness before, hunting together on the floor of the desert in the sacred place between the Four Mountains, the place of the Dineh? We go out, you and I alone, at the first light of dawn, bare-chested, our bows over our shoulders, catching the first glint of the sun above a purple pass far in the distance, walking softly, crouching, listening more than seeing, I sense you beside me, beautiful youth, love of my heart, quietly through the tall grass stalking.

In the flickering light of the campfire: your fine face with the high cheekbones, your hair down to your shoulders held back by a leather band, your strong arms, your brown hands clean now from a soaking in the stream. Companions of the hunt, we sit cross-legged across from each other smelling of wood smoke, chewing on a roasted hare, silent. Wordlessly, my eyes tell you how much I admire your prowess, your ability to become the deer with the white tail, to run with it. I smile at you. You see me and smile back, then lower your eyes modestly to the charred meat. Your legs, when you move to stoke the fire, are sinewy and strong. Through how many lifetimes have I stared into your eyes before we drifted off to sleep, one ear to the wind playing in the grass? Son, brother, nephew, apprentice, friend, lover.

In the morning, the scent of rain on the sage mingled with our sweet perspiration as we stride this flat weed-churned basin between the faraway mesas, black against the bright suddenly sun-struck clouds, like white mountains in the sky: you at my side, you the young part of me. I brush your arm and it is like being shocked by lightning. You motion to me that you are going to run in pursuit of something you heard, something you saw—or was it merely the shadow of a sparrow darting over a thicket of cactus? You disappear and I know heartbreak again. Will you come back? When?

Chapter Twenty-Three

Mike's parents were going to New Zealand to visit Mike's brother Billy and his wife Fiona that December, so Mike and I arranged to drive up to San Antonio to house-sit for them while they were gone and have a private vacation of our own. We wanted to use the time at Christmas to be away from San Miguel, our clients, our routine, even our friends. Both of us were tired from the hard work of the past few months, Mike with seeing often five or six people a day for body work, me with promoting *God On Your Own* and counseling clients.

I had thought we both were experiencing an end-of-the-year fatigue. After two or three days, though, Mike's energy had returned. He was out and about, shopping, visiting with relatives, meeting some new people. But I was still tired. When he wanted to go out to a movie—all the new films were coming out then, the week before Christmas—I suggested we just watch something at home, then fell asleep on the couch in the middle of the afternoon as the movie blared on. I woke up in a blur, trying to reenter the movie's story, which, I realized after a long time, was a second movie Mike had put into the DVD player after the one we were watching ended.

Before we left Mexico, Beverly told me it might be a good idea for her and me to take out modest life insurance policies on each other for business reasons. If something happened to either of us, the other would be able to pay off any encumbrances our retreat business might have. I agreed. She arranged for me to have a physical examination done at the house in San Antonio. On the day of the exam I got up and went to the gym, but got off the treadmill before the usual time because I was out of breath and feeling out of sorts.

The physical was conducted by a tough-looking woman in her mid-thirties with short blond hair who looked like she might have been a waitress at a Texas truck stop before becoming a medical assistant. I could imagine her pushing the lemon meringue pie at one table and at another pointing to the sign above the booth: "We reserve the right to refuse service to anyone." She was pleasant, but thorough to a fault. Blood pressure, urine specimen, blood sample, weight, height, eye test, long lists of symptoms with little boxes next to them, three pages of family medical history. After she left, I made sandwiches for Mike and me, ate half of mine, and took a nap. I was exhausted.

I did not know it at the time, but this Christmas season would mark the start of an *annus horribilis*—a horrible year—during which Mike and I would be put through a physical and emotional ordeal such as we had never experienced, and hope never to experience again.

Annus horribilis. I was in London in December 1992 when, a full two days before Christmas, the tabloid newspaper *The Sun* scandalously published a transcript of Queen Elizabeth's Christmas Message. Scandalous because the queen's annual message had always been reserved for broadcast at three o'clock on Christmas afternoon, when British families were gathered around the dinner table, respectfully prepared to hear a few uplifting words from the symbolic leader of the country.

The Sun's preemptive publication of the speech was the cruel addition of insult to the injuries of what the queen described a month earlier as her *annus horribilis.* "Like many other families," she said, in a masterpiece of understatement, "we have lived through some difficult days this year." In March, her son Andrew separated from his wife, Sarah; a few weeks later, the tabloids ran pictures of Sarah at the beach, topless and kissing a new boyfriend. In April, the Queen's daughter Anne divorced her husband, Captain Mark Phillips—an enormous embarrassment to the Queen, who holds the title "Defender of the Faith and Supreme Governor of the Church of England."

A month later the book *Diana: Her True Story*, a devastating exposé of the princess's doomed marriage, bulimia, and suicide attempts, was released world-wide. In November, Windsor Castle caught fire, destroying many irreplaceable works of art and causing millions of pounds of damage to the building. Finally, in early December, her son Charles, Prince of Wales, next in line to the throne of England, formally separated from his wife, Diana.

Along with several million stunned and amused Londoners, I eagerly bought a few copies of *The Sun* that day. But I felt a pang of guilt walking back to my flat, as if by buying the paper and reading the Queen's speech ahead of time I was adding to her misery, making her year even more horrible.

The incident of the scooped Christmas Message was not my first encounter with Queen Elizabeth. I had a run-in, almost literally, with her in London a few years before her horrible year. I was strolling pensively along a street in Westminster when a heavy iron gate opened loudly a few inches behind me. As I turned, I was practically swiped by a shiny black sedan rolling toward the main road. Through the side window a flat-palmed hand waved robotically from a wrist, and behind the hand the half-smiling face of the queen. I waved back, still slightly shaken; the car had come so close, I could see the reflection of my own dazed face in the fender.

༄

Thursday, January 17

I have waited till today to call the Medical School in San Antonio to make an appointment with a doctor there for an evaluation and probably a biopsy. I put it off until tomorrow. Meanwhile, I have begun to feel better. I have not taken the Xatral, the medicine to open my bladder, but my pee stream is stronger. I notice that I no longer have the raw, irritated feeling at the tip of my penis.

༄

Two Years Before

For Mike and me in San Antonio, Christmas came and went. A few days after we returned to San Miguel, we found out that I had been denied insurance because of the results of the physical exam. Two weeks passed before I was actually able to see the results, which were considered confidential and the property of the insurance company. When I went through it with Mike, everything was fine except for my liver readings, which were off-the-charts bad: I had Hepatitis B.

Now I knew why I had been so tired in San Antonio and why, even getting back to my exercise regime at the gym in San Miguel and watching my eating and drinking, I was not able to raise my energy level. I needed, in fact, to stop exercising entirely and start resting—physical activity was exacerbating the condition. By February, I was in bed most of the time, night and day.

Mike looked after me, bringing me magazines and movies to pass my time, but they sat on the nightstand untouched; I was too tired to do anything but sleep. I moved around only to go to the bathroom.

Whole days would pass without my venturing out as far as the living room of our apartment. When Mike was at work, our housekeeper, the saintly, maternal Belen, freshened the bed every day and made me *consome de pollo con ajo*, a clear chicken broth with garlic and a sprig of cilantro, but the soup bowl usually ended up cold on the windowsill by the bed as full as when it had come steaming hot from the kitchen.

During this time I began to drift into a kind of delirium, so that the boundaries between days and nights were blurred for me. Sometimes I would wake and look at the clock and not know for a few moments whether the time was telling the daylight or the nighttime hour. I imagined that since Mike was not in the room, he had left me and gone back to the United States. Why would he want to live in relationship with an old sick man? What was in it for him? I did not blame him for packing a few things in the black canvas suitcase—the one that used to be up there at the top of the closet, but now was gone, leaving the line of our luggage up there looking like a smiling, mocking mouth with a tooth missing. Had he taken the bag down or had Belen been dusting up there and moving things around? No, it was gone—he was gone. Had he taken all his clothes, or only what he needed for a week or two? I wanted to get up to go through the shelves in the closet, the drawers in the nightstand on his side of the bed, but…but I did not want to get out of bed right now. I would do that later, after I rested more.

Yes, surely, I would say to myself, those black shoes he bought in Centro, the ones from Leon with the square toes, are not here—surely he is wearing them on the bus to the airport. Look, his sweater, the brown one with the zipper all the way up to the top of the collar, is nowhere to be found and his keys—where are his keys? His school books, usually stacked on the desk in the spare bedroom next to his notebooks and the tan test books with the thin black cloth binding, did he put them...where? On the couch, on the shelf under the television set in the armoire? Did he take them with him in his green backpack when he walked quietly out of the apartment just before dawn, closing the door upon a note to me he left on the kitchen table?

Then I would wake up in the dark and feel him next to me, asleep, breathing open-mouthed like a child. He had not gone.

Chapter Twenty-Four

In mid-March, a month after I had taken to bed, I decided to go with Mike and Beverly to Tepoztlan, south of Mexico City, near Cuernavaca. Beverly had been ailing that winter, as well, and wanted to see Cofe, who was one of our visiting practitioners at LifePath Center. Usually he came to San Miguel once a month, but needed to stay in Tepoztlan this March. So we went to him for healing, which included a diagnosis with applied kinesiology and treatment with Chinese herbs.

When I left the apartment that morning, descending the thirty-eight steps to the huge door that opened onto the street, it was the first time in more than five weeks that I had been outdoors. Holding onto Mike, I walked to Beverly's waiting car half a block away, got into the back seat, and in a few minutes, as we drove up the hill to meet the highway, I nodded off to sleep holding Mike's hand.

The miracle of Cofe's healing method is that when the muscle-testing diagnosis is super-accurate, and it usually is, the herbs he gives as the remedy work almost immediately, within a day and often within hours. I saw him in the late afternoon, soon after we arrived. By seven in the evening back at the hotel, sharing a supper with Mike, I was feeling completely myself again, as if I had never been ill. The next day I went for a walk, the first walk in so long, through the streets of Tepoztlan. I had come alive again.

"I love seeing you like this," Mike said to me the next evening as we strolled down the main street of town that led out to the restored massive 16th Century former convent, with its huge buttresses and elegant arches.

"I was feeling so old and useless."

He grabbed me by my shoulder and drew me to him. "Not so useless—let's go back to the room and play." We had not made love in a while because we both were being cautious about the health of each other. The last thing I wanted was for Mike, who had suffered so much with Hepatitis that first year in Mexico, to have to deal with it again. He was immune to the A strain, but not to the B, my condition. Back at the room, we rediscovered one another again, this time with a heart-melting tenderness in Mike I had not seen before.

We never found out how I had contracted the disease, which is the case, I learned later, in about half of the people who get it. Cofe asked me during my session whether anything had changed in my general environment to bring my immune system down to the point where something like Hepatitis B could take root. I told him I did not know of anything. For several weeks the question of my weakened immune system remained a mystery.

When we got back to San Miguel the day after Palm Sunday there was a phone message from my sister-in-law. My brother Michael was not doing well; in fact, he was sinking rather quickly. Something else: a day after we returned, I felt my energy ebbing again—not to the low level it had been during my worst times, but lower than it was in Tepoztlan when I was with Cofe. I resigned myself to what was apparently going to be a back-and-forth healing, and drifted back into the old routine of reducing my activity, taking naps in the mid-morning and mid-afternoon, avoiding alcohol, and watching my diet.

The stress of knowing what my brother was going through at the same time did not help me feel any better. The next day I phoned him to cheer him up. We talked about the past, about growing up in our little town, about our parents and their foibles. I got him to laugh. But I felt exhausted and depressed, and I knew he, at the other end of the line, was feeling the same, and terrified at his impending death: two brothers, empty of energy, feeling alive by the thinnest thread, bravely propping each other up like two casualties of the combat of life.

"You have no idea," Michael said to me, getting serious. "They have to come and get me in an ambulance to take me to dialysis. Then they put me on the machine, which is torture. And after that, I go home again in an ambulance. It takes me all the next day to start feeling better. The day after that, I go back to dialysis." His voice was hard, biting the edge of anger. "This isn't living—it just isn't living."

"Hang in there," I heard myself saying, not quite convincingly.

"I don't know how much longer I want to do this." His voice trailed off.

I was silent. What could I say?

When Mike came home he found me curled up on the bed. Strong orange light from the spring sunset pressed through the thin *manta* drapes—natural cotton, the most common cloth in Mexico, and the most beautiful—onto the glowing walls. He stretched out next to me and held me.

"It's your brother, isn't it?"

I nodded, on the verge of tears. "I miss him already," I said. "I'm so sorry he has to go through this." In my weakened state, with my liver damaged by a disease whose origins were still a mystery to me, I could have been talking about myself.

Mike made a pot of tea and we moved to the living room to discuss what we should do. In my condition, I probably could not go to Ohio alone, or go at all. Mike said if I wanted to travel up there he would come with me. We would ask one of our friends to stay at our place, take care of Milly and the cat. We could start looking at airfares.

"Why do you think I am having this health stuff right now?" I blurted out, a strange thing to ask, as if the thought had come from another person. During the many weeks of my illness I had persistently asked myself *what* I had and *how* I got it—but never *why*.

"I think it's because you love your brother and on some level you have decided to suffer along with him."

I was startled at his comment. "Are you saying that I may be causing myself to be sick?" The minute I asked the question I knew the answer was yes.

"I don't mean you are doing it consciously...but it's clear to me that you have a connection with him that's showing itself in this way." His face softened into his "it's-all-okay" smile.

"Hum, so I'm making myself sick to show my love for him," I said, chewing on the thought.

Mike poured himself more tea and took a bite of a sugar cookie from the bakery down the street. On his way home he had bought a bag of sweets for the two of us, but not even my favorite cookie with the *limon* flavored frosting looked appetizing.

"Now that we know what's going on, you will probably get better," he said.

"Yes," I agreed, still thinking over what he had said. The following week a second opinion—or maybe a supporting opinion—about my condition came from Cofe, and it was just as surprising. He had returned to San Miguel to see clients and was set up in his office at our Center amid a dozen open cardboard boxes of white plastic bottles of Chinese herbs.

"I'm picking up some kind of electromagnetic energy in your cells," he said, continuing his testing by touching the tops of my hands with his fingertips, then pulling apart a loop he made with his own thumb and forefinger. "You said you were feeling much better in Tepoztlan, but you started feeling bad again when you got back home. I wonder if there is something in the apartment that could have lowered your immune system. Electrical appliances, microwaves?"

"Like a microwave oven? We have one."

"No, like something that would send out electrical waves...a transmitter, a..."

I stared at him for a moment, trying to process the new information that was flooding in from both of us. "Our apartment is under a radio tower," I said.

Cofe's face, serious and intense up to now, thawed into a smile. Then, thinking I may have been joking with him, he lifted his eyebrows and said, "Really?"

"Really."

"I knew it!" he said. The rest came together quickly. It was Mike who put in the final piece of the puzzle. He remembered that during the previous October the radio station next door had doubled the power of its signal, the better to reach the people out in the *campo*, poor farmers and ranchers who depended on the station as their only means of staying in contact with the world outside their remote areas and, by using limited signal phones, of communicating with one another. The station not only had increased its power, but had anchored its antenna's extension piece by cables that were attached to the roofs of neighboring buildings, including ours. In fact, the tower's new cable had been fastened to the roof right above our bedroom.

"Can you move?" Cofe said, reverting to his serious expression.

I felt my heart sink. That apartment had been our refuge and our love-nest. We had found in its age and dignified beauty a connection to Rome and my own family roots, and to Colonial Mexico. But I knew Cofe was right. Clearly, the electromagnetic field created by the radio station tower had been interfering with my health. When I told Belen about it she wiped her hands on her apron, thought for a moment, nodded, and said simply, "*Yo siempre fui cansada en esta casa*—I was always tired in this house."

Mike knew how much I loved living there, but he was more concerned about the health issues it was raising. "Don't worry—we'll find a great place," he said as we sat and talked on the little balcony patio with the pots of night-blooming jasmine we had put in when we moved there. "I just want you to be well. We have each other...we can be happy anywhere we live."

"The thought of moving right now leaves me exhausted." I was still feeling the effects of the hepatitis, getting around somewhat but taking long naps in the afternoon to try to restore my energy.

"I'll do most of it," Mike said, "and our friends will help." When he saw the concern in my face, he added, "Look, I know you can't even imagine what it would be like to have to pack boxes and furniture, and carry them down the steps and across town, but we really can't stay here."

"Right now I feel so old," I said, reaching across the table to hold his hand. A heaviness was welling up in me, an engulfing wave of sorrow. I sighed deeply to hold off crinkling up into sobs. I could tell Mike was reading my feelings on my face, and that made me more ashamed.

"Joseph, you're not old—you're recovering from a serious illness. Remember how you helped me? How you did everything for me because I couldn't do anything but walk to the bathroom to pee?" He pulled my hand to his lips and kissed me there, then rested his cheek on my open palm. "So let me do this," he said.

Almost robotically, we began to amass cardboard boxes and started packing. Mike worked at the office all day; I stayed at the apartment, continuing my convalescence. Belen did the heavier packing while I sorted through four years of accumulated bits and pieces of our lives. I wanted to get as much done as possible at home while he was away, but I kept running out of steam after an hour or so, and had to lie down. An hour before Mike returned to the apartment, I got out of bed and doubled my efforts to make it appear I had been working all day and contributing to the overwhelming effort at hand. He must have known my game because once he said, "It might be better for you just to rest and get completely well—don't feel that you have to tire yourself out to get all this done."

"I'll do what I can," I said.

"I'm going to move us. It's better if you save your energy and get well, don't you see that?"

I was not seeing anything clearly. He meant that he wanted me to take care of myself so that I would be back in good health, but I took it as a kind of scolding. Ashamed that I was still sick, unable to match Mike's stamina and pull my weight with the move, I felt myself slipping deeper into depression.

On Friday the *Atencion*, the English-language weekly newspaper, came out with listings of houses for rent. We combed them carefully and made calls. On Saturday and Sunday we looked at places. Few of them were suitable—they were either in the "wrong" areas of town or had less space than we needed, were too expensive, or did not take animals.

Finally, the second and third floor of a home in San Miguel's best neighborhood came up for rent. It was a Mexican family house gradually vacated over the years by several children, who had married and moved on leaving their mother with more space than she needed or wanted to maintain. The mother was a petite woman with hair dyed a becoming auburn, pleasant and accommodating, and, it seemed to us, eager to have human life back in the house—her only companions appeared to be a collection of perhaps a dozen birds, which she kept in a large long cage in the little courtyard outside her kitchen on the first floor. These were not exotic birds, but common doves and pigeons and grackles from the *campo* or from around town.

We signed a rental agreement and made plans to move in. Later in the day, we called our *patróna* and gave notice on our beloved downtown apartment. With a mixture of regret and excitement, we returned to our cardboard boxes of books and clothes and dishes, and continued planning our move.

That day was my brother's fifty-ninth birthday. I had phoned in an order for a cake from the local bakery in Ashtabula and our cousin Rosemary delivered it to him in the morning—white cake with white frosting, his favorite. It would be his last birthday, of course, as we all knew, so the cake must have had a peculiar resonance in the house, a sign of the celebration of life on the eve of death.

The next morning Michael called me to thank me for the cake and said how much he enjoyed it. Later, my sister-in-law Joyce told me he had taken a bite, smiled, then set it aside. I thought I was prepared for what he said next, but apparently I was not because in the short space before he pronounced the words I felt my entire insides rise up. Maybe we are never prepared for these things until they unfold in real time.

"I've decided to take myself off dialysis," Michael said in a voice I thought sounded strong and clear under the circumstances, almost robust.

"I see," I said, trying to come up with more words. He did not wait for me to react, but went on.

"From what I understand, if the toxins are not drained off, I have a week—ten days, max." It was his cop-voice, issuing a report in blunt, technical language. Max. He waited for me to say something.

"I respect your decision," I said finally, feeling my heart crack. "I'll make my travel arrangements. I want to be with you."

"I'd like that," he said. Then, maybe to fill the silence, as if confessing something that had been on his mind a long time, he blurted out on the edge of anger, "I wish I could just fall asleep and wake up dead!"

There did not seem to be much else to say. Given the gravity of his situation, I certainly was not going to second-guess him or judge him in any way, although technically he was choosing to end his life. We made a few short attempts at conversing, then we said good-bye.

Again the peculiar parallel of this time: the loss of my brother, the loss of our home, both occurring at the same time. In a kind of daze—I was not completely well, still—I bought my airline tickets and pulled some clothes out of some already-packed and ready-to-move cardboard boxes and folded them in my suitcase.

Mike found me in the bedroom over the open suitcase, hazily trying to decide whether to take two pair or three pair of black socks. I looked up at him and my eyes must have asked, "What is happening? Why is it happening?" He came to me and pulled me to his chest and held me there. In my exhaustion, I felt as if I could have gone sound to sleep in that warm place below his shoulder.

Chapter Twenty-Five

How many times through all these lives have you sat at my bed and held my hand and watched me take my last breath? Have you always been the young one, or have we changed places back and forth so that our souls could experience our love from both sides, now younger, now older? How many times have I sat at your bed and held your hand and watched you take your last breath?

How will the Angelo della Morte *come for me, as now he comes for my brother, gathering him into his arms and taking him away with a great rush of wings? Will you stare then, awestruck, unmoving, at the essential human mystery as I do now sitting here at the deathbed of my fraternal flesh and blood.*

Were we brother monks somewhere long ago, you and I? I seem to remember pacing slowly past the cool shadows of columns in a cloister, reading my Psalms to myself, seeing you suddenly turn the corner, catching sight of your exquisite face, feeling a longing far beyond the vague attractions of God and heaven, a blow so strong to the place below my heart that, as you go by I become weak and must look for a bench to sit on. Was the scent that enveloped me in that moment like an ambush of grace only the jasmine clinging to the shade-side of the campanile wall, or was it the perfume of our love, forbidden, unexpressed, delicious?

I am the apothecary of this monastery and you are a young monk training to be my assistant, learning the names of the herbs, studying the four humors, mixing tinctures, drying blossoms in the sun, grinding buds and seeds into powders. In the morning we go out together with our leather bags into the fields to gather fresh yellow hypericum perforatum, *this being the Feast of St. John.*

Olhe isto, irmão *I say to you, crumbling the petals of the first flower between my thumb and forefinger to release the fragrance. You lean down to smell my gold-flaked fingers and I glimpse your green eyes, your fair face framed by waves of ink-black hair, and above your lip the tomentum of youth, like the soft frost of hairs on these leaves. We are in the fields outside the Mosteiro de Pombiero in the village of Pombiero de Ribavizela in the council of Felgueiras, in the district of Porto in Portugal.*

Isto é uma nova flor, *you say—but of course it is not a new flower for me.*

Sim, para você, *I say, but gently because in truth it is new to you. I stand too quickly and become unbalanced. You reach out and hold me up until I regain my footing. In my mind I go to my last hour on earth, to the bed in the whitewashed cell with the crude wood cross on the wall which has been my home and my seat of contemplation for sixty years. I have received* Viaticum *and now, in the late afternoon, feeling myself sinking with the setting sun that squints through the narrow window, you are kneeling next to me holding my hand. I will never leave you, I will never leave you, I will never leave you.*

For me, the blessing of that week at my dying brother's side was the rare opportunity of reconnection. Over the years, we had stayed close through the mail and the phone, and more recently though email, but I had visited "home" infrequently, and when I did, I had not spent much time with him. Now my time was his completely.

He had taken to the guest bedroom, where Joyce had a hospital bed brought in. But rather than lying down, which would have constricted his breathing, he preferred to sit up on the edge of the bed. When he felt comfortable enough and rested enough we spoke about events from our childhood. I asked him questions about family history, sorting out the names of distant cousins and the themes of long-forgotten feuds. I knew the answers to most of the questions, and he must have known that I knew, but I was trying to keep him present, attempting to perpetuate the bond between us for as long as possible.

His condition deteriorated a little more each day. Since nothing was being done to intervene between him and death, his every breath was now part of a morbid count-down to the end. The hospice people came. The priest from Our Lady of Mt. Carmel church came and administered Last Rites; Michael had not been a regular churchgoer for years, and held a skeptical attitude about religion in general, but he had been a faithful altar boy all through grade school and high school, and he retained what we all hang on to at the end, I suppose, from the spiritual beliefs of our childhood.

We sat side-by-side on the bed all that last day. Sometimes I talked to him about the day—it was Friday, a rare beautiful May day out the window, fresh with the scent of lilacs—and, every hour or so, told him the time. In the silent times, I just held his hand. His eyes were closed the whole time; he had stopped speaking the day before. He ebbed hourly, until, at last in the early evening he took one long draught of air, let it out slowly, smiled, and relaxed lifeless back against the wall. I held onto his hand the whole time. Joyce, sitting at his other side, gathered his head in her arms and kissed him goodbye.

Within the hour, I got myself together, snuck into the other bedroom, and phoned Mike in Mexico. "I'm so sorry," he said. "I'm glad I got to meet him. How are you dealing with all this?"

"I'm fine. Everything's fine." Actually, it was. My brother's death was in a way a great relief—for him, after years of suffering, as well as for all of us. "It's good to hear your voice…it's a comfort." There was a flutter of activity in the living room; the undertaker, a man I had gone all through school with from Kindergarten to high school, had arrived with his son to take my brother's body away.

"I have to go," I said. And then, as a quick afterthought, "Are you okay—everything getting settled there?"

Chapter Twenty-Five

"Yes, don't worry. I'm going to be sleeping tonight in our new place. I'll kiss your pillow goodnight. Everything's fine here."

I could not know that at the other end of the line a drama was about to play itself out that would impact both of our lives deeply and bring our relationship to the brink of separation.

The next morning in Mexico, Mike woke up for the first time in the new apartment. It had been a night of disturbed sleep because of incessant chirps and chatters from the landlady's birds in the cage below the bedroom window. He got out of bed at five, finally, and rummaged through our still-boxed belongings to find earplugs. Once he began unpacking, he continued, laying things out on the floor, then putting them away in drawers. The birds went on, even louder and more insistent, he thought, as the day broke.

He spent the rest of the day exhausting himself by unpacking more boxes, finishing the painting he had begun earlier in the week, hanging ceiling fans, and getting the satellite dish connected. Workmen and friends with helping hands were in and out all day. He crashed on the bed around ten at night, hoping that he would be able to catch up on the rest that had been denied him the night before. But, with the hubbub done and the people gone, the bird sounds became more audible, until they seemed to him to take over the entire place. He moved the bed into what we originally designated the guest room, farther away from the birds in the courtyard, but the sounds traveled down the hall and through the closed door to torment him.

Utterly fatigued, he drifted off to sleep as the birds prattled on. In the morning he was awakened by the birds shrieking at the rising sun. As he told me later, he lost it. He began screaming himself, hurling curses at the birds, at the landlady, at everything that had conspired to bring him to this place, a room acrid with the smell of drying paint, cluttered with boxes and strew with clothes, echoing with the unrelenting sharp sounds of birds.

"Stop it! Stop it!" he yelled, holding his hands over his ears, tears of anger and frustration streaming down his cheeks. "Cover up the cage, you idiot! Cover the fucking birds so they'll stop!"

The ruckus in the upstairs apartment roused the landlady, who was dressing up to go to church. Terrified, she locked herself in downstairs and picked up the phone.

Later that Sunday morning in Ohio, Joyce and I were picking out a casket, getting my brother's burial clothes in order, buying a plot at the Catholic cemetery. As the day wore on I was on the phone with high school friends who called with condolences, trading stories of recent deaths in their own families and sharing their own aches, pains, and ailments, which they nonetheless generously dismissed in the face of my loss. We continued making arrangements: calling hours would be Monday evening; the Funeral Mass would take place on Tuesday morning.

In Mexico, Mike had calmed down from his outburst and was trying to decide what action to take.

First, he knew he needed to talk to the landlady and get her to agree to cover her birds at night. Such a conversation would require better Spanish than he had, so he called Eduardo, who has come in from Tepoztlan to conduct a healing workshop at our center. When Eduardo arrived at the apartment a few minutes later, he and Mike went downstairs to speak with the landlady and found her flanked by her three grown sons, who appeared as angry and protective of their mother as baited pit-bulls.

She would not cover her birds, Mike reported to me a few hours later. Furthermore, she thought the rental arrangement would not work. It was a bad match. She wanted us out as soon as possible.

"My screaming must have scared her," Mike told me on the phone. "She was freaked out. But so was I...I just couldn't stand the terrible noise."

"Well, better for this to happen now than a month from now," I said, trying to put the best face on the situation. "I'm sorry about all this."

"I'm the one who's sorry. Oh, Joseph, I had everything ready for you...I had the cable connected and the phone set up and...and...I was going to have the bed made, and roses..." he started to sob, something he rarely did. I knew from his surge of emotion that he was thoroughly exhausted—from the work of the move, from the stress of having to deal with the Mexican family, from lack of sleep.

"God, I wish I was there to help...just to be with you," I said.

"I know, I know. You need to be there." He was trying to regain his composure. "I love you so much.

I wanted everything to be done and perfect, so you could just come home to a new place and rest… and we could be together…and…" He broke down again.

We spoke for a few minutes more. He would take the rest of the day to plan the move out of the apartment. He would need to rent a storage space somewhere in town, pack everything again, and move it all there. Friends would help. Beverly, who had stayed on top of the unfolding events, told him we could stay with her for as long as it took to find another place.

Meanwhile, I was writing a eulogy for Michael, which he had asked me to do before he began sinking into the darkness the week before. I wanted to be in Mexico with Mike, but I wanted to be here, as well, completing my duties to my family at this critical time of passage, hoping to heal the areas of my heart left ruptured the loss of my baby brother. My body was in Ohio, but my mind was in Mexico with Mike. My emotions were all over the place.

A numbing sleep fell over me that night. With my parents and my brother dead, I was now truly an orphan. With our new apartment lost—later Mike would call it "the four-day house"—I sank into a kind of hopelessness.

Here, hold my hand and let me tell you this: do not be afraid—we are players in a drama of our own authorship, and we move from scene to scene convinced of the truth of it all, this masterful theatrical we have devised for soul learning. None of it is true, and yet all of it must be experienced as if it were. And so we stumble, you and I, shoulder-to-shoulder, down these paths and across these bridges of the life we share willing to suspend our disbelief for each other's sake.

Remember when we were walking across that bridge in the jungle, you going before me, musket in hand, and the rope that had been soaked by the late summer rains and rotted through gave way and you lost your footing? ¡Soy perdido! *you cried, as you stumbled on the slats. Remember how I found superhuman strength in that instant and reached out and encircled you with my maille-clad arm, an arm that appeared from nowhere—how I held you trembling in my arms and pressed you to my armored chest, brother of our battles?*

This is like that.

Chapter Twenty-Six

Friday, January 18

On this sunny afternoon, Mike and I have lunch at an outdoor café in Centro, three blocks from our offices. I tell him I am feeling good—so much better than I had been feeling for a month.

As the girl takes our orders—we are craving chicken *alambres*, a version of *fajitas*, but with more chilies and onions—we chat about the day, our schedules, everything but my problem. Finally I ask him, "What would you think if I don't make an appointment with the Medical School in San Antonio?"

Mike pulls a warm corn tortilla out a small round basket lined with a cloth napkin and fills it with some of the *alambre*. "That's your choice," he says after a pause.

Then, as if he has been thinking about this for a day or two, he says, "We've been going down this allopathic medical road from when the problem started. I'm just not sure why we are doing all these things with doctors and hospitals and pills and biopsies and..."

"You're right," I say. "We both should know better—we both know better."

"For a couple of days now, I've been asking myself, why have we bought into the whole sawbones medical system? Why haven't we been walking our talk?"

Suddenly, I feel both ashamed and relieved. I agree with him. I should have remembered, I say, that I studied for several years with Hazel Parcells, a pioneer in the field of natural healing, and wrote a book about her and her methods, which were both unconventional and highly effective. I should have remembered that there would be other ways to diagnose my condition and treat it.

"And I should have remembered that for six years I have been studying natural medicine," he says. "I have a degree in Natural Health, and in a few weeks I'm going to be a Doctor of Naturopathy."

By now we are sipping hot espressos, our "dessert," and they feel good going down because for a few moments a cloud races across the sun on this January afternoon and, amazingly, the temperature drops by that seems like ten degrees.

"We were afraid," I say, draining my cup. I look up at him questioningly, then down at the cup, suddenly feeling like an embarrassed little boy.

"Yeah," he says, nodding his head. "We were afraid."

Chapter Twenty-Six

Saturday, February 9

I get up at seven and, without eating or drinking, drive my motor scooter down to the little laboratory in Centro to take a blood test for prostate. This time, a young man is on duty. He finds a vein in my right arm immediately, and takes my blood effortlessly and, for me, painlessly.

༄

One Year Before

I left Ohio the day after the funeral physically and mentally worn out. That morning at the Cleveland airport I was sent off by Mary Lou, my date at the senior prom almost half a century earlier. "You look like you're seventy-five years old," she said with her usual bluntness mixed with compassion. I did not have the energy to laugh at her half-joke. I kissed her goodbye and shuffled to the security gate, wearily remembering that I would need to take my shoes off for the security people, longing to curl up in my window seat and fall asleep.

I arrived back in San Miguel to a confusion of changes. We were all now crowded into one bedroom in Beverly's second-floor apartment, Mike and I, Milly and Madre, and stuffed in with us two large suitcases packed with enough clothes for a week or so—we had no idea how long we would be "between houses"—cardboard boxes filled with things we needed for everyday, shaving kits, towels, a laptop computer, vitamins in plastic bottles, creams and lotions, shoes: just organizing the room took nearly an hour.

Milly, who, as she turned ten, had begun to sprout white hairs on her previously all-black belly, must have assumed we were on holiday with "Auntie Bev," and adjusted to the new situation easily; as long as she was with us, she was content. Madre the cat, almost two years older than Milly, had a harder time trying to find a place to nest. Eventually she claimed her property by curling up atop a cushion that we had stashed on a box by the window.

Beverly's day-bed was two single beds, one rolled under the other. At night, we pulled the bottom bed out from under the top one and made up both of them in the small space on the floor from which we had cleared our things by stacking them in temporary piles around the room. The beds' heights were uneven, of course, so when put together there was a mattress-sized step between Mike and me. That was a symbol, I thought, of our mental and emotional states: we were out of step with each other, out of synch, and disconnected. We held each other's hand for a few minutes before we dropped off to sleep, but it was not enough somehow. I wanted to feel his body next to mine all through the night as I had for so many years. Even our occasional furtive lovemaking in those cramped quarters seemed once-removed and unsatisfying.

"I feel like we're being tested," I said to him after four days, during which I had precious little time to process the fresh wound of my brother's death. We were folding the beds up and making some space in the room to spread out some things we needed from our boxes.

"I'm feeling the same thing—and I'm not sure I'm going to pass this one," Mike said with a humorless chuckle. He was out of the apartment before I felt the full blow of the remark, but it haunted me the rest of the day.

A friend of ours in San Miguel who had made retreats with us in the past phoned the next morning. She had heard through the grapevine that we were between homes and, since she and her husband were leaving the next day for Peru for six weeks, we might want to stay at their place. They had a house-sitter coming in from Austin, but we could stay in their guest casita. I felt my shoulders drop and the worry-wrinkles in on my forehead relax. Six weeks.

We moved over to their house, a tastefully remodeled and exquisitely furnished Colonial in Centro. When the house-sitter did not arrive at the expected time, we tried contacting her, but without success. Finally, the next afternoon, we got an email letter from her saying that she had suffered a panic attack on her way to the airport and had to go back home. But she would try to come the following day. She never showed up, so as it turned out we were returning a favor to our hosts by staying there and taking care of the house and the dog while they were gone.

Having some space to ourselves, even though it was not ours, helped Mike and me to feel that we had a life together again. But the events of the past few weeks had a shattering effect on our relationship.

I wondered whether he blamed me for being away during his traumatic move of our household, blamed me even for having been susceptible to the radio waves at the old apartment—in which case, he would be blaming me for my age. For my part, I was having trouble getting above my irrational resentment over having to move out of the downtown apartment, or at least having to move out so quickly. Mike sensed this—it was never far from the surface of my thoughts—and might have been resenting my resentment; whenever we were in public and I mentioned the word "homeless" as our current domestic status, I could see him out of the corner of my eye doing a slow-burn.

Communication, which we had always prized above every other value in our relationship, seemed to have flown out the window. We spoke to each other every day, went out together every evening, slept together every night, but our deep bond was missing. Our connection had become unplugged.

One warm afternoon, after returning from Centro to collect our mail, I sat in the shaded patio of the house where we were staying. Milly was asleep at my feet, having spent an obligatory few minutes growling up at the neighbor's elderly Rottweiler who was patrolling his roof next door.

I was paging through a *New Yorker*, but not really reading it. I was having trouble concentrating on anything longer or more involved than a cartoon caption. My brother had been dead for about three weeks by then, and we were two weeks into a house-sit that was going to last at least for another month. Our lives had settled down somewhat, but I was still in a fog from it all, mildly depressed and distracted.

When Mike got home, he came out to the patio and played with Milly for a few minutes, then walked over to me. Almost immediately, he turned away and started walking back into the house. But he stopped, and strode over to me. I peeked at him over the top of my magazine. His expression was dark.

"You are always hiding out! You hide out in magazines, in books, on the computer…." He locked on my eyes with a concentrated gaze. I had never seen him so serious or so angry.

He sat down across from me, still holding his stare. "Why do you do this? Do you even know that you do it?"

I must have been staring back at him in complete puzzlement, because he forged ahead with his accusations, his voice rising. To me, this outburst seemed to come out of nowhere. I was speechless.

"You don't tell me what you're thinking—and I'm not a mind-reader. You pull away from me all the time. It's like I can't reach you." He let out a low moan, like a hurt animal. "I hate this!"

As if on cue, the old Rottweiler on his rooftop perch was aroused from a daydream by something in the street below and began to bark in a kind of rage. He scrambled up to the edge of the roof and snarled, then took up his thunderous barking again. The sudden sounds surrounded us and electrified our confrontation. Then, just as suddenly as the commotion had begun, it was over.

We were silent for a few moments. I searched around in my head for something to say, but was not able to grasp at anything. His rant seemed to have emerged out of thin air, but I knew deep within me that it had been stewing in him for a long time. I also knew he was right: I had disconnected myself from him many times, been secretive with my feelings, closed down and closed off.

"Look, Joseph, if this is what you consider a relationship, I don't know if I want it," he said. His face was tight, his expression intense. "We don't have a house to live right now," he said. "I've been thinking that maybe I should get my own place, and..."

My heart seemed to stop. I felt a sudden rush of anxiety as the blood drained out of my face. If he leaves me, especially now in my weakened, vulnerable state, I told myself, I will die. Just that: I would have no reason to continue living. I listened to him and, as I looked at his face, it was like I was looking at the face of a stranger.

"Mike, I'll do anything.... What do you want me to do?" I asked him quietly, my eyes lowered.

"Stop hiding from me."

Words, possible words, caught in my throat. I knew I hid myself from Mike, but I did not know how to stop it and do my life differently. My shame over loving young men, ironically, had led me to conceal myself from the young man who loved me.

We talked on haltingly, with long pauses, into the early evening. I tried to assure him that I still loved him and wanted to continue this relationship that we both had put so much effort into over many years.

I said I would like to see a therapist to help me over my grief and depression—and my way of concealing my emotions. Then I started shaking softly and felt a tear slip out of the corner of my eye. Was it the prospect of Mike leaving me or the fresh memory of my brother's death or being uprooted and homeless that was making me cry like a child? All these, I suppose.

"I don't know why I go into hiding," I said, speaking to myself as much as to him. Over the years I had become a professional at hiding. I had hidden my sexuality and my sexual preference from my family, my colleagues, everyone.

Then, as if the dawning insight were being pushed up to my brain on the wave of these emotions, I said, "Maybe...maybe I have been pulling myself away from you because I want to protect myself from the possibility of losing you. Yes, I think that's it. All these years I have been terrified that you would leave me. I love you so much. Just thinking that you might go away and never come back makes me sick to my stomach."

He stared into my eyes for a long moment. At some point we had begun to hold each other's hands. As we sat looking at each other, light left the patio. From the rooftop next door the Rottweiler let out a low growl for no apparent reason, then circled around in the nest of an old carpet and settled down with a long sigh.

"When will you get it?" he said. "When will you understand that I love you?"

"I know that, but..."

"And I'm not going anywhere," he said, punctuating his declaration.

I did not feel the tear that Mike now leaned over to wipe off my cheek. I did not feel relief or release or elation. I only felt a tremendous sinking weariness, the echo of the shame of my age, because although Mike may not be going anywhere, I, dragging the burden of my years behind me up the hill of this relationship, surely would be leaving him in a few short years.

I looked gratefully and longingly at him, his expression now soft and boyish. He came around the table and sat on my lap. We ended the day in each other's arms, listening to the cicadas caught in the blood-red bougainvilleas on the back wall near the fountain.

Those few hours had been wrenching and exhausting for both of us. In the morning, we woke up holding onto each other in the first crimson flush of day and began the process of repair.

Lying next to you now, two years later, waiting for sleep to descend upon us, I whisper to you that you are my life, that I love you above anything in this world, that you are precious to me, that you are my Michael. You murmur back from the edge of slumber, I love you, my Joseph... very much. The music we are falling asleep to is a soft flute air from somewhere. The melody takes me to Arcadian hills I never knew in this lifetime, where I stand on a cliff looking out at a ship leaving the harbor below, its sails catching a quick strong gust to take it out. You are beside me. Are you my younger brother? my son? my student? I see from the astrolabe you are holding that you are learning navigation with the star-taker. You may have passed some test or succeeded in some experiment, because I turn to you and place my hand warmly on your shoulder, and from this you know how proud I am of your accomplishment. The hint of a certain musky scent plays around your thatch of golden hair: frankincense oil. Without my seeing it, while I was attending to other things, you became a man.

Chapter Twenty-Seven

By the start of summer, Mike and I were established in a new place in San Miguel, a huge eight-bedroom house that we shared with Beverly—and with people who were making retreats with us, and Eduardo and his family, Cofe and his family, and other of our visiting LifePath practitioners who needed lodging when they were in town. We loved the living situation, but we both were hoping for the day when we would have a home that was just ours, a house that we would build and own.

Meanwhile, we had a fine house and a compatible little community of like-minded and like-hearted people around us, starting with Beverly, who over the years had become so much a part of our lives that having her close by in the next room seemed entirely natural and appropriate.

Monday, February 11

In the evening, I return to the lab and the girl behind the counter hands me the results of my blood test results in a white envelope. I pay for it and, before I am out of the building, tear the envelope open and pull out the report, which is printed on heavy paper and signed by the technician. My PSA is at 6.1, a full 10 points lower than it was a month earlier. Cofe's herbs have worked. As a wave of relief washes over me, I realize I am feeling better now than I have in months.

In the afternoon, Mike and I drive our scooters over to our gym, a well-worn facility with old, but sturdy workhorse machines and weights. The owner is a gringo friend of ours, a cheerful white-haired gent who looks like he might have been nicknamed "Coach" by generations of lifters in the States and, later, here in Mexico, where he is semi-retired; the staff is all young Mexican men and women. The place has the feel of a pleasant neighborhood club.

Feeling a surge of new energy, I hop on the treadmill and start my work-out. The gym membership was Mike's gift to me at Christmas; every time I look at my little orange laminated membership card, I silently thank him. That Christmas day in San Antonio seems like a lifetime ago.

I speed up the treadmill belt and stare out the window at a sunny, fine early spring afternoon in San Miguel. Some of the trees are out. In a couple of weeks big lavender blossoms will bloom on the *jacaranda* trees, which in the winter looked dead but, as we can clearly see, are alive.

༄

Six Months Before

Once settled, all three of us wanted to take a vacation from the events of the previous couple of months. We had wanted to travel to Cuba since moving to Mexico seven years earlier. The idea of experiencing it now, before the inevitable transformation that would take place with the passing of Fidel Castro and his regime, appealed greatly to us. In July the opportunity came up, and we made the trip—Beverly's two daughters joined us from the States.

"You are a *terrible* traveler, do you know that?" Mike said the second night in Havana. "Ordinarily you're great, but on this trip you're a pain."

He was right. I was moody and complaining and distant. I found Cuba lifeless and depressing, and turned even those few things that were exciting and interesting about the country into shortcomings. Havana seemed like a slum to me. Old Havana, the city's partly restored "old town" section, was somewhat colorful and lively, but in a forced way, it seemed to me. The weather was painfully hot and humid.

What I hated most, beyond the empty stores and markets and the secret privately-owned restaurants, was the obviously demoralized populace, most of them hanging out in what looked like bombed-out buildings with nothing to do. With the collapse of the Soviet Union, which had been Cuba's main supplier of spare parts and building materials, the island country began to fall apart for lack of simple maintenance. There were few doors on apartments, fewer windows; streets and sidewalks had huge gaping holes, and some streets and sidewalks just stopped in peculiar places, as if marking where both the supply of concrete and human motivation ended.

I found Cuba a poverty-stricken police state, like a tropical version of East Germany twenty years earlier. It boasted that every citizen received a free education—but what on earth were they learning? And that everyone was given free medical care; from the looks of it, no one in the world needed medical care more than these poor people, ravaged by scarcity and plagued by malnutrition.

Mike and the others enjoyed themselves, I thought. But I, still smarting from the emotional lashes of the year up to then, pulled in my head like a turtle and endured.

ဢ

Wednesday, February 13

I have a follow-up session with Cofe. "The cyst is diminished by 40%," he says matter-of-factly. I show him the results of the lab test and he is pleased with my PSA reading of 6.1.

"Good—yes, this confirms what I am finding. I am picking up only a small amount of bacteria in the prostate. That should go away with the new herbs I'll prepare. Now we'll treat what's left of the cyst to dissolve it completely."

He mixes up a new batch of Chinese herbs for me and tests the dosage with his finger-tip method. As before, I am to take one small spoonful four times a day. My gratitude is boundless. Our eyes meet over the plastic herb bottles and, wordlessly, Cofe accepts my thanks.

Am I to be a professional curmudgeon, then? Will you dismiss me as a crabby old recluse and leave me in my room, checking on me from time to time, shaking your head and clucking your tongue. Will you drive away, then, shrugging your shoulders, sorry that you ever got involved, disgusted at having wasted so many years of your life on so ill-considered a project as our "relationship."

Be patient with me. The clouds of my desolation soon pass and there you are as the last mists burn away, waiting. When, in sleep, I wrap my arm around your waist and pull you more closely to me and press myself against you, I feel in that moment the blessing of some wise god who has bestowed upon us the illusion of immortality, so that this brief parenthesis in time can be our eternity of love.

I grow older, but in this cupped-out instant, I am young again in you, and you are younger still. Where our love is, there is no time.

∽

Monday, March 31

Today I have another session with Cofe. According to his testing, the cyst is almost gone; the inflammation in the prostate is gone, as is the bacteria. I am in good health.

From the lab, I have learned that the PSA reading has dropped again, to 4.5.

༄

Four Months Before

Early in September, a piece of land became available in the country about ten minutes from San Miguel. We bundled Milly into the car with us and drove out to see it.

"You stand right there," Mike called out from the far end of the lot, where he was making his way to a crude marker, a large rock with a splotch of red paint on it. "So, it goes from where you at the road are to here, then from here…to the end of that fence" He was stretching his arms out in a ninety-degree angle, marking the far corner of the property.

"It's beautiful!"

"Just look at these views!" he said, sweeping his arms now around the hilltop plot, vast stretches of open desert valley going south all the way to the *presa*, San Miguel's lake, formed by the damming of the Rio Lata, and west to far-off ranches. Five kilometers to the east was San Miguel, the lights of which we would be able to see at night, and behind it a jagged mountain range, a deep purple setting for the twinkling diamonds of the town, on its way north to San Luis Potosi. The land all around churned with tall green grass at this time of the year, at the tail end of the rainy season. Huge cactus formations and a few old mesquites rose up in an otherwise vacant landscape. The sky was everywhere in that place; standing there, high up as we were, we felt a part of it, like birds.

Mike ran to me from his post at the outer edge of the lot and wrapped his arms around me.

"I'm so happy," he said. "I'm so incredibly happy to be doing this with you."

I held him for a long time in the baking afternoon sun, then we broke our embrace to gaze out on the land again. Someday, the gods willing, we would make our home here.

We signed the papers for the land on the afternoon of my sixty-fifth birthday. It was the first piece of land either of us had ever owned. For weeks, I had been having difficulty with my impending landmark birthday, at first not even wanting to acknowledge it or mark it in any way. Both Mike and Beverly thought it strange that I would not want to celebrate the day, but in my mind, still frayed by the events earlier in the year—the hepatitis, my brother's death, the loss of our apartment—it was another reminder that I was inching closer to decrepitude and death, inching farther away from the arms of my life's true love.

"Let's celebrate getting the land, instead" Mike suggested. "That way it will be the birth of something else, too—not just your birth, but the birth of us as *rancheros*. I managed to do that, but I was sullen for a week afterwards. A manila envelope had arrived a month or two earlier from Social Security announcing still another birth, the start of my life as a Medicare recipient. Finally I opened the letter with its chirpy "Welcome to Medicare!" cover letter, and sunk back into my depression.

My disposition lifted as a glorious autumn set in. Mike's parents came to visit, giving us more reason to be out and about in town, extending the celebratory mood that had begun when we bought the land. When the parents saw the property, they loved it as much as we did. Before they left, we made plans to stay in their place in San Antonio over Christmas, while they went to visit Mike's brother and sister-in-law in New Zealand.

I was still sluggish and despondent from the year that was quickly coming to a close, my *annus horribilis*. And yet I could not know that one day in early November, perhaps a week after *el Dia de los Muertos*, unknown to me and without my feeling anything, a bacterium of mysterious origin lodged itself in my body, descended over several days through my body, and wedged itself in slow stages into my urinary tract, and from there made its way to my prostate gland, the seat of my sexuality.

My horrible year was not yet over.

༄

Chapter Twenty-Seven

Thursday, April 3

Out the bedroom window on this late afternoon in spring, the branches on the Jacaranda trees in the park are swaying in the breeze, casting shadows on the curtains. The whole room seems to be cradled in a tree house. I wake up early from our nap together and, washing my face, look at myself. I am aging by softening. Yesterday someone sent me a photo of myself taken a year ago and I stared at it as if staring at a stranger. Even a year ago I look older than I imagine myself to look now. A softening, a kind of melting of my features is happening. My hair is somewhat whiter and thinner. Do I look sadder or more tired than I did last year?

Later, at the computer, I send to a friend in the United States the photo that was taken of me a year ago here in Mexico. I send it out without saying the photo is a year old, that I am now a year older than I was then.

I look back into the bedroom. Shadows of the trees in the park outside our window have begun to appear on the gauzy curtains. Mike sleeps soundly, like a child. His face in repose, relaxed, in another world, shows no lines or creases. Watching him, my mind turns: When he is thirty-seven I will be sixty-seven; when he is forty, I will be seventy; when he is forty-five, I will be seventy-five. How much time is left to love him?

I close my eyes and, as I float into a quiet nap I am back in a dream of a few months ago. I am walking at night in the garden of a mansion. Cool blue moonlight streams through the trees, but otherwise it is dark. I am walking down a narrow path between tall weeds. Feeling the urge to masturbate, I start feeling myself, hoping that no one will pass by. But then, up ahead is a man and he is coming toward me. He is bald, fit, a determined look on his face. I zip up my pants and begin to retrace my steps back to the mansion's patio, but now the man is upon me. I am terrified. I stare him square in the face, plucking up all my courage to do so. But, to my surprise, he does not see me at all. He walks right past me without turning his head. I watch as he strolls away down the path as if in a trance. He disappears into the shadows.

Chapter Twenty-Eight

May 11, 2008

A year has passed since my brother's death. I decide to mark the day by going to eight-o'clock Mass at the *Parroquia*. Instead of driving my scooter, I walk down to the center of town, making my rare church attendance a kind of pilgrimage. The Mass seems both familiar—how many hundreds of Masses have I sat and stood and knelt at?—and remote, as if I had never been a believer; remote, too because it is said in Spanish and I am translating from Spanish back into Latin, and from there into English.

After Mass I eat breakfast of *huevos rancheros* at the little restaurant under the portal at the far end of the *Jardin*, finishing with a small piece of white cake, Michael's favorite. On the way back to the house I feel close to him, so close that at one point I begin to converse with him. I miss him.

We are planning to take a LifePath retreat group to Bali in September. Today I learn that we will be leaving from Los Angeles for Bali, with a stay-over in Hong Kong, on September 16, two days after my birthday.

May 16

I am combing the Internet for news and I see that in California the State Supreme Court has ruled that a decision brought by a lower court to ban marriages between same-sex partners is unconstitutional. Legal unions between same-sex partners will begin in California a month from today, on June 16.

I email the article about it from the *New York Times* to Mike with a two-word comment: "How great."

May 25

"*A*s long as we're going to be in Los Angeles in September..." Mike says. It is morning and we are in the *sala* that adjoins our bedroom putting on our shoes.

"Yes?" I say with a long drawl. I have a feeling about what might be coming next.

"I thought that as long as we're going to be in L.A., we could, you know, get married."

"Really? I mean, is that something you would like?" The subject had never come up before, not seriously. We had kidded about it, and cheered on states and countries when news arrived that same-sex marriages had been made legal there, but we never discussed it as a possibility for ourselves.

"Yes, I think so," Mike says. "Let's do it."

I have tied my tennis shoes and get up off the couch. Then, heavily, I sit back down again. "Married," I say, feeling a little out of breath. "I'd like to think about it."

Later that morning, I go into Beverly's room where she is working at her computer. "I think Mike has proposed to me," I tell her, still somewhat unclear about how I feel about the brief exchange Mike and I had.

"Oh?" she says with a smile, as if she has been waiting for us to make the connection between the travel dates and the California Supreme Court ruling that she made a week earlier. "And did you accept?"

I grin back at her and tell her the truth. "I told him I would think it over." We both explode in laughter.

Later, while Mike is at work, I continue my conversation with Beverly, expressing my reservations about getting married. She leaves her desk and sits on one of the two wicker chairs in the sitting area of her large bedroom, and motions for me to take the other chair.

"We are not professional homosexuals," I say. "We don't march, we don't go to Pride celebrations, we never send in petitions or write to our congressmen or join support groups or raise money for same-sex causes. We're quiet people, and we consider our sexuality normal and private. I'm thinking that for us to get married might be misconstrued as being a political statement. It's just not something we stand for."

Sophie, Beverly's spunky cocker-spaniel drags one of her toys, a stuffed frog doll, under the coffee-table between us and chews on it quietly. "I disagree," Beverly says. "Everybody who would know about your wedding also knows who you two are and what you believe in."

"What I believe in, and what I think Mike believes in, is not to push our sexual preferences and our age preferences in people's faces." After almost a decade of knowing her, I feel that I can talk to her as I would to a sister—and she is more to me and to Mike than that. She listens to me carefully, catching every word as she would in a counseling session with a client.

"Look, Joseph," she says after a moment, "it might be a good idea for you to be public about your relationship. Maybe it's time for that."

I realize while she is talking that I may be carrying the shame of my sexuality with me still after all these years. But, I know in a crystal moment, there is no reason to feel ashamed of myself or of Mike.

"Besides," Beverly goes on in her best calm psychologist voice, "marriage doesn't have to be a political declaration or anything like that. Marriage is an open, public declaration of two people's commitment to each other in sacred relationship. Marriage is an archetype."

She has been doing this with people for over thirty-five years, I remind myself, and so I am not surprised that she has cut to the core for me. *An archetype.* With my love for Carl Jung and Joseph Campbell, how could I possibly resist that?

Chapter Twenty-Eight

September 14

Mike and I marry in Los Angeles on my sixty-sixth birthday. We have chosen a hotel near the airport for the ceremony to make it easy for family members and friends to fly in, stay over, and return home quickly. It is also an easy destination for anyone in the Bali retreat group to attend, since the Los Angeles airport is our embarkation point. About fifty people, including some of my old Hollywood pals, make up the celebratory group.

"Hey, you're pacing the floor," Mike says to me in our hotel suite as we are getting dressed in our black pants and white *guayaberas*, traditional Mexican wedding shirts. "You're going to wear out the carpet. The last time I saw you like this was when you met my parents for the first time."

"Aren't you, like, nervous?" I ask, daubing at my perspiring brow.

"No, not at all. I'm really enjoying this."

I roll my eyes and let out an edgy little laugh. "Youth!" I say.

My dear old friends and lifelong Californians Pancho and Maggie are my witnesses, Mike's much-loved Aunt Judy and his mother's octogenarian foster-mother Betty are his witnesses; Beverly is our Matron of Honor. My family is represented by my lovely cousin Camille Licate, an actress who splits her time between New York and here. Miraculously, I choke up only once during the ceremony, when I end the reading of my vows with, "…and I promise to love you all the days of my life."

Mike has made our identical plain gold bands from the "leftover" gold pieces his jewelry teacher Andi gave him when he left Las Vegas and moved in with me in Santa Fe. They are simple gleaming rings. I am still so nervous that I try to force Mike's ring onto the ring-finger of his right hand. When it will not get past his knuckle, he holds out his left hand, starts the ring on the correct finger, and guides my hand to finish the job. "Try it this way," he whispers, looking up at me and stifling a laugh.

At the reception after the ceremony, Bill and Sharron lift heartfelt toasts to us, and Bill gives a moving salute, enjoining his dear son and me to be fruitful and productive in our marriage by finding creative ways of contributing to the lives of others. His words are so touching that for a moment a respectful silence falls on the crowd.

Mike and I dance to Linda Ronstadt's rendition of "My Funny Valentine," which lyrics seem singularly appropriate—

Thou knowest not my dim-witted friend The picture thou hast made Thy vacant brow and thy tousled hair Conceal thy good intent Thou noble, upright, truthful, sincere And slightly dopey gent...
You're my funny Valentine.

For all the apparent normalness of the occasion— the exchange of vows, the kiss that seals the ceremony, the reception line, the banquet, the wedding cake, the toasts—this is still a peculiar event: two men, thirty years apart in age.

The uninvited guest at the feast is Time. We all feel its presence and we all seem to accept it philosophically.

Two days later, we flew to Denpasar, the capital of Bali, Indonesia with a group of twenty-three LifePath retreatants, many of whom had attended the wedding. The three-week excursion to the other end of the planet, to magical, spiritually intoxicated Bali, was our honeymoon, but also a work assignment—a LifePath Retreat Journey. Both Mike and I tried to concentrate on the business at hand, he leading Yoga exercises and I conducting dreamwork groups, but while our heads were on our tasks, our hearts were bound up in one another.

The trip, following so closely upon the wedding, seemed to extend the sacred character of what we had undertaken. It was as if the public declaration of our union had allowed us passage into the paradise of this remarkable place, with its temples on every street corner and its flower petal-and-water offerings to the gods on every doorstep.

After the main group left Bali for home, some of us stayed behind for another week. On one day six of us took a bicycle tour of an area around Ubud that began at the top of a mountain. Our guides drove us up the mountain in a van and we bicycled down through the entire day, stopping at small villages and farm houses and rice paddies along the way. It was a grace-filled day, my lover peddling alongside me through this remote and exotic countryside, discovering new vistas over the next hill, discovering thrilling new places within each other, as well.

֍

December 8

The cardboard tube arrived at our mail service in Centro a week ago, but Mike was in Austin, visiting a naturopathic doctor who was using an energy healing machine called the Asyra System. He was considering getting something like it to redirect his practice away from body work and more toward naturopathic counseling. When I saw the tube, I knew before I read the return address that it was his diploma naming him a Doctor of Naturopathy. All the years of study, all the scores of term papers and examinations, all the calls and letters back and forth with his advisor, all the nights after work studying, the weekends—they were all rolled up here in this humble mailing tube.

When he got back from Austin, I told Mike I wanted to take him to dinner to talk about his experiences on the road. We went again to the same New Orleans-style bistro with the white tablecloths that had seen so many of our send-off and welcome-home celebrations. On the way in, I slipped the mailing tube to Alejandro, the jolly maître-d, and whispered that he should bring it to the table with dessert at the end of the meal. We sat in our usual place, by the crackling fireplace, and talked and talked.

Dessert was delivered on cue by not only Alejandro, but his whole crew of starched white-shirted waiters, all of whom we knew by name, lighting a candle they had plunked onto the top of a big wedge of chocolate truffle cake and singing "Happy Birthday." The tables around us joined in.

"Whose birthday is it?" Mike asked innocently over the racket.

"Not mine," I said. "It must be yours."

"My birthday was in May...oh, my God..." Alejandro handed him the tube just as the song was ending. "Oh...my...God." He blew out the candle and one by one the waiters shook his hand and patted him on the back with gentle *abrazos*.

"What did you wish for?" I asked him when the hullabaloo subsided and we were alone again. He was smiling and shaking his head as he carefully unwound the wrapping from the tube and slid his diploma out: *Michael Charles Herbert, Doctor of Naturopathy.*

"I wish...I wish I will be able to help a lot of people with this."

As we dawdled over espressos and the rich dessert, other diners, catching the news, came over to the table and congratulated Mike. The fire in the fireplace had burned down to jewel-like embers, and so had the evening. He took my hand and held it across the table briefly in a moment of silent gratitude—he thanking me for supporting him through the long process of his education, me thanking him for living up to the promise I saw in him so many years ago.

We got up to leave and, as Mike was rolling up the diploma to return it to its protective tube, he looked at me—but spoke to someone else, someone who was not in the restaurant, or even in this world.

"See, Grandpa...see? I did it!" he said.

November 27, Thanksgiving Day

*O*ur Mexican friends acknowledge it as *Dia de Gracia* for us, but it is not celebrated as a holiday in Mexico, so today is a regular work day here. While we are at home downtown with a gathering that includes our co-workers and neighbors around a long table loaded down with the traditional Thanksgiving dinner, a gang of construction workers arrives at our land in the country. Soon a backhoe chugs up the hill, crawls past the open gate, and moments later ground is broken on our house.

Mike designed the floor plan first on paper napkins and the backs of envelopes, then transposed the sketches to typing paper, and finally onto graph paper. From that point our architect took over. He told us it would take four months to build. To ourselves, Mike and I doubled that, adding on another four months—this being Mexico, where, as our old landlord Manuel once told us, *mañana* does not necessarily mean "tomorrow," just "not today." Then we allowed for a month or two more.

We know there will be delays—rain, rock where there should have been soft soil, materials that do not arrive, water trucks that get lost on the back roads of the campo, workers that do not show up because of fiestas we had not known about.

We do not care how long it takes. We have time, we have time. And it's going to be a fine house.

Once, when we were on the bank of the Tiber watching the river rushing to Ostia; once, when it was near sunset the Temple of Vesta gleaming in the light such as we had never seen before—you turned to me troubled and with enormous wonder—as if you were coming awake finally out of an ageless sleep. You turned to me and in your eyes I saw the halls of eons. I speed down those halls into the heart of your soul. We had union in our eyes. I remember this as if it were the day before yesterday. I kissed your eyes. You held my hand and would not let it go. For hours you held onto me—while the sun set, the stars came out, night settled around us, the damp of dawn.

Now I remember those very long, deep hallways into your soul, down which I traveled to find you—alone, a pilgrim in your world. Alone, and yet somehow united with you, a part of you. We rode to Ostia the next day, you at my side. We had to oversee the grain shipments from the South. I could think of nothing but you. I felt your hand at my side as we boarded the ship and I knew a strange sensation—as if all this had happened before: all of it. I see a lock of your black hair fall across your forehead in the breeze and I feel that I will die—because the beauty of you is so much to bear. I half-faint, barely catching myself. Your beauty dazzles me and makes me weak. I think that this bond of souls goes back farther in time to when we hitched lions to our chariots and rode through the desert to see the great pyramid of Kufu, already seventeen years in the building, being completed—the one side plastered and glimmering in the hard sunlight, our faces glowed in the light. You have a band of gold around your forehead holding black locks back. Your tunic is feathery light linen, like silk—white with an indigo border. You are of the royal family: a favorite nephew. You are my nephew, my treasure. I watch you grow from spirited boyhood to sturdy and confident young manhood. I see the delight you take in your beautiful body—I catch you feeling your flat stomach, your hairless chest, so full now with definition, so hard, and yet yielding to the appreciation of your hand. The scent of lavender surrounds you—and the smells of pleasure oils. You have come just now from bathing with other, younger men, and you have the aroma of manhood about you, like myrrh. Your skin has a gold glow from within. You are studying the sacred mysteries: how to harness energy, how to make objects disappear, how to stop time, how to transport yourself from one place to another without moving, how to affect people's thoughts and actions with your mind. When I catch you in your self-worship like a young god, you laugh, showing me your wonderful white teeth and I laugh with you, for I was young once, and will be young again. Your eyes connect with me like a key in a lock and suddenly you know—you know all the lifetimes we have been companions. You know me and I know you. To me you are like the reflection of my own face in the mirror. I see myself when I look at you. We are going through ages together—golden gods finding each other in these myriad lifetimes.

I look down at my feet to see my mandarin red slippers, then I look up to see your eyes—straight, slanted now in this palace in Old China. You are a novice scribe: you have just learned how to place characters in rows to make both accounts and stirring poetry. You came in from watching the gold carp in the reflecting pool. You are scented with frangipani and I also smell orange oil on you. Your beauty is remarkable to me. I want to be quiet in its presence. Beauty such as yours calls for contemplation. You disrobe with me to enter the pool and I see your young limbs again. We stare at each other in the water, naked, water up to our chests. I am moved by your beauty, fascinated. Your eyes move over me until they catch at my eyes and we remember other lives, other times. How I love you! How receptive you are, how charged with life. How much you know. How much you remember. Remember, then! When I embrace you, I hold you down the ages, through the thousand life stories of our souls. Our soul, for indeed all are one. Do nothing. Simply be. The universe is making something of the space between us—the rich manna that can feed the multitudes, for love is like food. Take this and eat of it, for this is my body. Love is the fire and the flood. It is the end of the world—and the beginning.

The time of the gods is returning. Pan is in the forest—strange winged creatures have been seen in the mountain passes. I can hear the hypnotic harp of Orpheus. The gods are among us. And we are them.

Afterword

April 2009: In a Mexican Monastery

The Grand Silence has descended upon us, the period between the chanting of the holy hour of Compline, the last hour of the day, until after Mass the next morning. I remember the Grand Silence from my own monastery days, an interval so solemnly quiet that only the most compelling emergency could break it. Cowls are pulled over the head, lamps are extinguished, the world stops.

The monks are shuffling softly down the hall toward their cells to retire. The sun dropped behind the mountains less than an hour ago, but they must be up at three-thirty in the morning and in the chapel to sing Matins and Lauds, the first liturgical hours of the day. They will begin:

Lord, in the morning you shall hear my voice
And in the morning I have prepared myself to appear before you.

I have been here for a week, dwelling with *los hermanos*, the brothers, in silence and prayer, eating their simple meals with them, working alongside them in the fields, which in this hot and dry season are parched, sun-scorched. In the still afternoons, we have been clearing withered corn stalks from the hectare behind the barn.

Soon I will have to put my light out to join the observance of the Silence—even light during this time is an infraction of the rule. I am sitting at a small wood table next to my narrow bed, which is covered with pages from this manuscript, and reflecting on what I have read.

Some years ago, when the well-known homosexual writer and musician Paul Bowles published his memoir *Without Stopping*, never once revealing his sexual orientation, William Burroughs, his friend and fellow-writer, hissed in a review that it should have been titled *Without Telling*. I have been like that my whole life: not telling. Now it is told—not as shame, but as salvation.

I understand my spirituality to be inextricably bound to this relationship with Mike. It is here, in the arms of my beloved, that I have found my soul's center. This is my great spiritual school, where I am learning those values toward which my heart has always strived. Loving Mike openly has allowed me for the first time to feel that I am living an authentic life, free from humiliation and grounded on self-acceptance.

In this splendid school, I am discovering how to be generous, as I lavish my full attention upon him and freely offer him my most precious possession at this point in my life, time. I am being taught patience, as when things do not go exactly as we had planned or when one of us missteps in some way—patience in waiting for the next thing he needs to say, in holding back from finishing his sentences or leaping to conclusions.

Together we are being taught the lessons of magnanimity, of courage, of mutual respect, of surrender, as when we entertain each other's opinions and treasure each other's insights and stay open to each other's movements of the heart. We are trying to live in alignment with the values of responsibility and frankness, and teamwork, as when we engage a project together and see it through to completion. We are cultivating the virtues of vulnerability and openness and serenity, as when we withdraw from conflict and relax into each other's embrace. Our iron-clad rule is to communicate. We consider ourselves equal to one another.

Through it all, we are feeling an emptying of the ego out of us as each fills the other with a love that is deeply human and also, in some mysterious way, divine. For God is Love, say the scriptures of the world.

In the matter of age, we seem to have embraced the archetype of the mentor-student bond that might be as old as time itself, my *erastês* to his *erômenos*, as the

Greeks had it—and they were not the first. Rather than apologize for the nature of this connection, I am seeing it now as exactly how it should be for me in this lifetime. No doubt we two have exchanged roles down the ages, my soul teaching his soul, then his soul teaching mine.

Toby Johnson, who writes brilliantly about sexuality and spirituality, and is himself a former monk, reminds me that this model of relationship often can be highly productive, stimulating creativity that can influence culture in a fundamental way. The mystical poet and anthropologist Edward Carpenter was forty-seven when he met George Merrill, who was twenty-five; Walt Whitman was forty-five when he met Peter Doyle, who was twenty-one. Lord Alfred Douglas was twenty-one when he took up with Oscar Wilde, sixteen years his senior; fourteen years separated film director James Whale (*Frankenstein*) and producer David Lewis.

In our day, the distinguished theologian Malcolm Boyd was sixty-one when he met activist-author Mark Thompson, who was in his mid-twenties; the researchers and authors of the groundbreaking "The Male Couple," Andrew Mattison and David McWhirter, were fourteen years apart. Toby and his partner are separated by fourteen years—he was thirty-eight when they met, Kip Dollar was twenty-four. Pioneering psychologist Don Clark was forty-six when he met Michael Graves, who was in his early thirties; novelist Christopher Isherwood was forty-eight when, on Valentine's Day in 1953, he met Don Bachardy, who was eighteen.

And the list goes on. Women examples, from Sappho and Anactoria to the present would require another whole long list.

As for past lives, would that not be a plausible explanation for two people from different generations meeting—finding each other *again*—falling in love, and promising to stay devoted to one another until the death of one of them? Is there such a thing as a soul-mate? Are there such things as past lives?

So much of what has transpired in the making of our love remains a mystery to me. I have stopped trying to analyze the psychology of it. I no longer theorize about arrested sexual developments, father substitutes, recovery of lost youth, sublimated biological need for progeny, issues of power, issues of submission, mutual exploitation, family-of-origin dynamics, dysfunctional cultural programming, and the rest.

I only know, after all these years, that I must be the happiest man in the world, feeling most of the time like Adam walking in the Garden with the Creator in the cool of the day. If it is true that, as Toby Johnson says, "the goal of any spirituality is to experience being in heaven now," then this love must be where the spiritual path I embarked upon in secrecy and shame so long ago has led.

Through the window of my small room I see lights going out one by one across the cloister where I imagine the monks are moving in slow-motion, folding back their narrow beds, preparing for sleep. The silence settling in now is a kind of huge and holy presence, like the soundless music of the stars that hover above this place, witnesses of our brave humanity, flawed, angelic.

Acknowledgements

I would like to thank everyone who is mentioned in this book for being part of the story of our relationship, particularly Mike's parents, Sharron and Bill Herbert. I am grateful, as well, to Toby Johnson for his insightful comments and suggestions. And to Beverly Nelson, Wade Ashley, Lynn Carlton, Winton Churchill, and Skye Wentworth for their wise advice after reading early versions of the manuscript. Thanks, finally, to my book coach, the gifted writer Eva Hunter, who helped me frame the material, and then held my hand through the process of writing and publishing.

About the Author

Joseph Dispenza is the author of several books, many of them about living a higher quality of life. Early in life, he spent eight years as a Catholic monk. After that, he worked for the American Film Institute in Washington, D.C. and Los Angeles, directing its education programs. Some years later he created a film school, the Greer Garson Communication Center and Studios at The College of Santa Fe (now the Santa Fe University of Art and Design). He then moved to Mexico and, with other wellness professionals, founded LifePath, a retreat center for holistic healing and personal growth in San Miguel de Allende. He is a spiritual counselor in private practice.

www.oldermanyoungerman.com

Book Clubs

If you are a member of a book club, or would like to start a book club with a group reing and discussion of this book, reading and guides are available to help the group gain a understanding of the subject matter. You arrange with the author to make an video-call appearance to your group to answer questions.

www.oldermanyoungerman.cc

Made in the USA
Lexington, KY
17 May 2018